made in india

made in india

Kunal Vijayakar

JAICO PUBLISHING HOUSE

Ahmedabad Bangalore Bhopal Bhubaneswar Chennai
Delhi Hyderabad Kolkata Lucknow Mumbai

Published by
Jaico Publishing House
A-2 Jash Chambers
7-A Sir Phirozshah Mehta Road
Fort, Mumbai - 400 001
jaicopub@jaicobooks.com
www.jaicobooks.com

MADE IN INDIA
ISBN 978-81-8495-641-2

First Jaico Impression: 2015

Printed by
Repro India Limited
Plot No. 50/2
T.T.C. MIDC Industrial Area
Mahape, Navi Mumbai - 400 710

DEDICATION

For my grandparents

Ayoomum – Pa

Aaji – Ajoba

from whom I inherited no riches, save for the
endowment of an impeccable palate, an abundance
of appetite and the wealth of their recipes.

ACKNOWLEDGEMENTS

I should have only myself to thank, because the amount of time, stress and stamina it has taken me to put together this small compendium of recipes is shameful. I'm not saying this is a great literary work, but I've literally had to slog to select and deliver these recipes. Since I am no chef, I could not conjure up dishes as I went along. Instead, I've had to delve into my beginnings, recollect my excursions, extract from my retentiveness and borrow from the classics.

Having said that, without these people, this book would never have happened:

I start with my mother. She kept me fed all my life, through fat and thin. She still does whenever I give her a chance.

Zenobia Boman Irani and Olivia Broacha, who open up their kitchens and their hearts every time I call.

All the cooks, *bawarchis*, housewives, restaurateurs and chefs who have slaved in front of fires for me; especially Chef Joy Bhattacharya, who will always be my friend in need.

Mohit Khushlani and Sakshi Anand, companions on my foodie trips, who wielded their cameras for fun and were kind enough to share some of those moments for the book.

Tarana Arora, who did all the dirty work, so that this book may be completed in time.

My cousin, Rahul Velkar, every kilo we've put on, we've done it together.

Prashant Godbole and Ram Mandale, for helping with the cover design.

Ayesha Broacha, friend and photographer, whose job was to make the food in the book look appetizing and me look delicious.

And finally, her husband, Cyrus Broacha, whose time I hope she will forgive me for monopolizing, but who remains my best food and drink companion to date.

FOREWORD

Kunal S. Vijayakar was born on May 19, 1964. He was a healthy, eight-pound, bonnie baby. This is also the only time in the English language that the word "healthy" and Kunal S. Vijayakar have been used in the same sentence. There were signs early on of his true calling. While other boys were playing cricket or football out on the maidans, Kunal roamed about asking for lunch. Kunal, and this is absolutely true, traces his ancestry to William the Conqueror, who changed the course of European history in the battle of Hastings in 1066 AD. William was known to eat four kilos of venison and drink ten glasses of wine everyday. Kunal can do the same and occasionally does. Proof, if any, that William Normandy lives today, albeit in a two-bedroom house in Prabhadevi, Mumbai.

Critics may argue this link on the flimsy ground that Kunal can't ride a horse or fling a javelin. But believe me, on all accounts, neither could the original.

Kunal's likes and dislikes are known to his friends. Let's start with his dislikes. At last count, there were over 40,000, ranging from watchmen in lifts to people in general. When it comes to his likes, his answer is simple. It's that four-letter word all parents with obese kids hate to hear, "food".

Granted that there are better chefs, perhaps grander connoisseurs, more accomplished culinary experts all over the world, but when it comes to passion for food, no one compares to the direct descendant of William the Conqueror. Here, there is no fraud, no deceit, no compulsion, just pure, unbridled, undying, unyielding love; a love more pure than a mother's love for her child. Keep in mind that Kunal is no parent. Not yet at least. A wonderful anecdote will warm the cockles of all our hearts. Once at a traffic signal, a poor, old beggar approached Kunal, who was treating himself to ice-cream. I gently prodded the great one to part with his ice-cream cone. Pat came the reply, "Share my butterscotch ice-cream?"

The day we share butterscotch is the day that heralds the death of civilization, and so, he ate on and he continues to do so. Inside this almanac are some of his greatest discoveries. Explore them and share the cuisine of a king. One who conquered Great Britain many, many, many years ago. Enjoy the proof of his unrelenting passion.

I'm often asked what Kunal's favourite dish is. Her name is Neha, but that's a whole other story and a much shorter book. I'll end with the words of actor-singer Farhan Akhtar, altered to suit our subject. If Kunal S. Vijayakar, resident of Prabhadevi, Mumbai, direct descendant of William the Conqueror, were to give a piece of advice to anyone, this and only this would be it: "Eat On."

—Cyrus Broacha

CONTENTS

Dedication	4
Acknowledgements	5
Foreword	7

VEGETARIAN   14

Dive into the sensational world of vegetarian cooking with this mouthwatering variety of dishes from across the country.

Brinjal Fritters	16
Tamilian Kotthu Paratha	18
Gajar Koshimbir	19
Bhindi Fatafat	20
Phodnichi Poli	22
Kashmiri Pundit Dum Aloo	24
Madras Onion Sambhar	26
Double Bean Sukka	27
Channe ka Pulao	28
Pakistani Dal Tadka	30
Sookha Vatana	32
Akki Roti	36

Scrumptious Akki Roti

Bhopali Roti	38
Varias	39
Aloo Paratha Tadkewala	40
Hingatelache Vatane	43
Goan Potato Curry	44
Pakoda Dahi Khadi	46
Charcharleli Batati	48

EGG   50

Scrambled, fried, poached or baked, eggs are a delight in every form. Experiment with these dishes for any meal of the day.

Akoori on Toast	52

Spicy Goan Egg Drop Curry

Esperanza's Chicken Curry

Pizza Sunny Side Up 54

Indian Scotch Egg Curry 56

Fugias 58

Goan Egg Drop Curry 60

CHICKEN 62

These easy-to-cook and fuss-free, creative chicken recipes use traditional spices and unique textures to thrill each and every bite you take.

Esperanza's Chicken Curry 64

Kaju Chicken Korma 66

Chicken Pasta Curry 70

Kori Chicken Sukka 72

Bombay Chicken Curry 73

Gomes Cafreal 74

FISH 76

You'll soon take to eating fish with a new fervour and gusto as you treat your tastebuds with these delicious sources of Omega 3, cooked in the flavours of red chillies, cumin and fresh and dried coconut.

Pomfret Moile 78

Prawns Atwan 80

Chinchoni 82

A fiery Chinchoni

Eddie's Mutton Stew

Fish Kujit	84
Prawn Pathwad	85
Prawn and Drumstick Curry	88

MUTTON 90

Die hard mutton lovers will enjoy these tender, flavoursome and succulent dishes.

Shikari Pulao	92
Kheema Paratha	94
Green Kheema	96
Abeda's Nihari	98
Egg Fried Mutton Chops	100
Mutton Do Piaza	104
Mutton Khuddi	106

Mince Potato Chops with Mint	107
Eddie's Mutton Stew	108

BEEF 110

Dig into these hearty and fragrant beef dishes from Pakistan, Kerala and Goa.

Pakistani Pot Roast Fillets	112
Kerala Beef Fry	115
Chorizro Pulao with Dry Fruits	116

DESSERT 118

Sugar, milk and khoya are staple ingredients to a festive spirit!

Pakistani Pot Roast fillets

Luscious Sev Badam Burfi

Sev Badam Burfi	120
Tipsy Pudding	122
Vanilla Sheermal	124
Croissant Pudding	126
Anday ka Halwa	128

SIDES 130

Add balance and delights to your meals with this selection of knockout side dishes.

Chutney	132
Ginger Garlic Chutney	133
Pear Chutney	135
Lagan nu Achaar	135

Pathare Prabhu Chutney	138
Panchamrut Drink	139

MASALAS 140

Flavour your everyday staples with these unique combinations of fragrant Indian spices.

Bottle Masala	142
Rechad Masala	143
Index	144

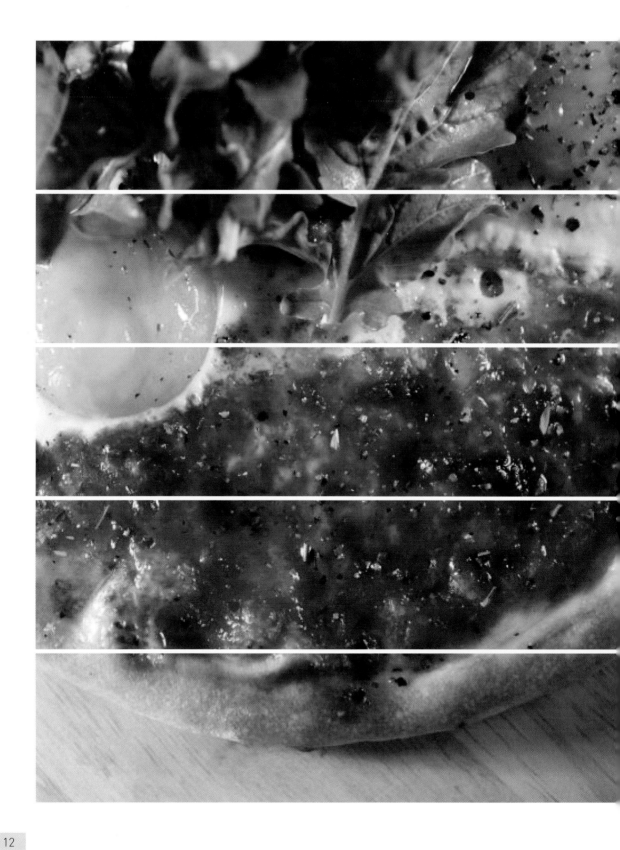

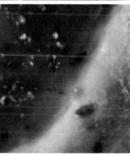
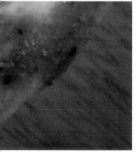
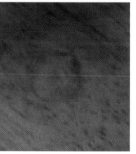

QUICK GUIDE

This book has been laid out to give you all the information you need before you embark on an exciting journey into the world of Indian cuisine. Kunal's personal notes and step-by-step guidance promises a fascinating cooking experience.

 This indicates the amount of time it takes to cook the dish.

 This indicates the number of people the dish can serve.

 This indicates other eatables the dish can be served with.

VEGETARIAN

Initially, vegetarian meant potatoes and green peas to me. At home, our cook had a repertoire of ten vegetarian dishes: two potato-based, two green pea-based, three dals and the last three were a mysterious-coloured salmagundi. My grandparents turned vegetarian on certain religious days, but then it would be Sabudana Khichdi or Shengdanyachi Amti (raw peanuts cooked in jaggery and coconut), neither of which had any greens. It was later as I made new friends and traveled to parts of Rajasthan, Gujarat, Punjab and Tamil Nadu, that I actually tuned in.

BRINJAL FRITTERS

You can fritter away money or time, but once you've 'frittered' brinjals, time stands still and even money can't buy its taste. Just kidding. This recipe gives you the simplest, tastiest way to eat brinjal. It involves practically no effort. The key is to slice the brinjals really thin and choose slightly firm ones that are just about to ripen. By the way, botanists hold that brinjal (or aubergine) is not a vegetable but a fruit.

Brinjal often has a slightly bitter taste. When cooked, however, it turns fleshy, absorbing large amounts of oil, butter or sauce and develops a rich, complex flavour. Salting and rinsing the sliced brinjal will also help reduce the bitterness as well as the absorption of fats.

RECIPE

 15 mins   Serves 3   mango pickle or chutney

INGREDIENTS

1 large brinjal, sliced into ¼-inch rings

2 cups rice flour

¼ tsp salt for batter

A pinch of turmeric

½ tsp red chilli powder

Oil for shallow-frying

Additional salt to sprinkle over the sliced brinjals

METHOD

Sprinkle some salt on the brinjal slices and set aside for 15 minutes.

Rinse and pat dry with a paper towel. In a bowl, mix the rice flour, salt and chilli powder together. Now coat the brinjal slices with the flour and masala mixture.

In a wok, heat the oil for frying. Shallow-fry the brinjal slices till golden. Serve hot, with a good Maharashtrian meal of Varan Bhaat and mango pickle.

TAMILIAN KOTTHU PARATHA

Instead of chucking leftover white rice, most homes use it in some sort of masala-fried version to be had at breakfast the next day. Similarly, when I was younger, unconsumed rotis were torn to bits and sautéed with onions, green chillies and spices to create a quick, tasty morning snack called Phodnichi Poli (see recipe on p22).

The Sri Lankans made an art out of the shredded roti. Muslims and Tamilians in Sri Lanka are credited with the creation of the Kotthu Paratha. Created in the 1970s, the recipe's popularity has since spread to Tamil Nadu. This shredded, flaky, buttery paratha is cooked with a pastiche of onions, chillies, tomatoes and veggies and spiked with rich masalas. It's street food at its best.

RECIPE

 25–30 mins   Serves 4–5   onion raita

INGREDIENTS

5 stale rotis, cut into small pieces

1 medium onion, finely chopped

2 large tomatoes, chopped

¼ cup carrot, chopped

¼ cup cabbage, shredded

¼ cup green beans, chopped

½ cup green peas

5 cloves

1 bay leaf

1 sprig curry leaves

1 one-inch cinnamon stick

1 tsp fennel seeds

2 tsp red chilli powder

½ tsp turmeric powder

2½ tbsp garam masala

2 tbsp ginger-garlic paste

5 tbsp oil

2 eggs (optional)

METHOD

Heat oil in a pan. Add cinnamon, fennel, cloves, curry leaves and bay leaf and fry for a minute. Then add ginger-garlic paste and fry till the raw smell disappears. Now add the onion and wait for it to turn a light, translucent brown. Mix in the tomatoes, along with a pinch of salt. Cook till the tomatoes turn mushy and oil starts to separate at the sides. Then sprinkle in turmeric powder, red chilli powder, garam masala and mix well. Cook for a minute.

Now add the beans, peas and carrot. When they are half done, mix in the cabbage and cook till it is soft (yet crisp). Add salt to taste and cook for another minute or two.

Then throw in the shredded rotis. Mix them well and stir occasionally on medium heat for 5–7 minutes. Garnish with coriander leaves.

If you wish, beat the eggs and cook them into the mixture till dry. Squeeze a little lemon juice over it and serve with raita.

GAJAR KOSHIMBIR

This is the closest you can get to a salad in Indian cooking. It is often said that the Koshimbir (or *kachumbar* in Hindi) is the sub-continental cousin of the salsa. This particular one is made with luscious raw carrots. Carrots are low in calories, healthy, packed with vitamins and really sweet and juicy if fresh.

A huge splash of tart, acidic lemon juice makes the Koshimbir tangy and refreshing. When tempered with just a wee bit of asafoetida, the taste of the dish is reminiscent of sautéed onion and garlic.

RECIPE

15 20 mins Serves 3–4 plain yoghurt and hot roti

INGREDIENTS

The Carrot Mixture

2 carrots, peeled

1 green chilli, finely chopped

4 tsp peanuts, coarsely ground

1 tsp lemon juice

2–3 tsp sugar

½ to ¾ tsp salt

Tempering

2 tsp oil

1 tsp mustard seeds

3–4 curry leaves

½ tsp asafoetida

Garnish

Grated coconut

Lemon juice

Coriander leaves

METHOD

In a bowl, grate the peeled carrots. To this, add the coarsely ground peanut powder, chopped chillies, lemon juice, salt and sugar. Mix well and keep aside.

Pour the oil in a pan. When the oil is hot enough, add mustard seeds and curry leaves. Let it splutter and then sprinkle the asafoetida. Pour this tempering over the carrot mixture. Mix lightly.

To serve, garnish with grated coconut, lemon juice and coriander leaves.

BHINDI FATAFAT

To me, ladyfingers (or okra, as they are also known) are controversial. There are the okra-lovers and there are the okra-haters. For many people, ladyfingers are gooey and slimy. But I know too many fans of the ladyfinger, who swear by the slender, green vegetable. In parts of the eastern and southern Mediterranean, where okra is hugely popular, they cook it without cutting, and by tossing it in salt and vinegar, allowing it to marinate for an hour or so. This makes it less slimy. You can also dry it in the sun after salting it. Back home, we fry a lot of *bhindi*, sometimes slicing it so fine that it turns into crisp fritters in the oil. However, if you like okra the way I suppose god meant it to be – soft, gooey and slimy – toss in onions as well, as shown in the recipe below.

RECIPE

 20 mins   Serves 4   hot chapati, or dal and rice

INGREDIENTS

500 gm ladyfingers

½ medium onion, sliced

½ tomato, diced

2 green chillies, slit

1 tsp mustard seeds

1 garlic clove, bruised

8–10 curry leaves

2 tbsp coconut oil

Salt to taste

1 cup water

METHOD

Remove the heads and tips of the ladyfingers and slice them diagonally.

Heat water in a pan. Add the sliced ladyfingers along with the onion, tomato and green chillies. There should be enough water in the pan to cover the vegetables. Sprinkle some salt.

Bring the vegetables to a boil and then simmer for about 6–8 minutes, or until the ladyfingers seem tender.

In a small frying pan, heat coconut oil, then temper with mustard seeds, garlic and curry leaves for about 30 seconds. Pour this tempering onto the cooked ladyfingers.

Cover and cook the dish for a few minutes more till all the water has evaporated.

Serve hot.

PHODNICHI CHAPATI

A simpler version of the Tamilian Kotthu Paratha (see recipe on p18), this Maharashtrian specialty is also made with leftover rotis. It is sometimes called Phodnichi Chapati or simply Kuskara, which means crumpled. If you don't have any stale rotis, you could also try this recipe with old slices of bread. In a variation of this recipe, you could replace all the ingredients with a little ghee, crushed jaggery and some sesame seeds. Combine these thoroughly with stale roti into a soft mixture and roll into small balls. Voila! You have a very tasty ladoo!

RECIPE

 15 mins   Serves 2   plain yoghurt or raita

INGREDIENTS

4–6 stale rotis

1 medium onion, chopped

2 green chillies, finely chopped

½ cup peanuts, roasted and ground

1 tsp mustard seeds

A pinch of asafoetida

1 tsp turmeric powder

1 tsp lemon juice

2 tbsp oil

Salt to taste

Sugar to taste

½ a cup of coriander leaves, finely chopped

METHOD

Tear the rotis into coarse pieces. Set them aside.

Heat oil in a pan and add mustard seeds and asafoetida. When the mustard seeds begin to pop and crackle, add in the turmeric powder, green chillies and curry leaves.

When the oil turns fragrant, mix in the ground peanuts and onion, and fry for a minute or so.

Now mix the shredded pieces of roti and fry for 3–4 minutes. Cover the pan and cook for a couple of minutes, till the mixture turns soft. (Otherwise, the dish will turn out crisp and crunchy.) Once cooked, take the pan off the flame and add salt, sugar and lemon juice.

Garnish with coriander leaves and serve hot.

So many choices, one destination. Pure vegetarian at Vishala, Ahmedabad

KASHMIRI PUNDIT DUM ALOO

I shudder when I see Dum Aloo on the menu of a Mughlai or Punjabi restaurant. It often comes as softened full potatoes, stuffed with dry fruit, in a thick creamy gravy, sometimes garnished with cashews and pomegranate seeds. It tastes slightly sweet like Shahi Kofta. Unfortunately, that's not what Kashmiri Dum Aloo is meant to be. Two Kashmiri Pandits in particular need to be mentioned here: Rajni Vanchu, a housewife who fed me a huge meal in Srinagar, and Chef Suman Kaul of ITC hotels. This recipe is Chef Kaul's version of Dum Aloo. Pandit food tends to be really spicy, often eaten with white rice to balance the flavours. Similarly, Kashmiri Dum Aloo is spicy, dry and leaves behind oil or *rogan*, which in Persian means clarified butter or fat.

RECIPE

45 mins   Serves 4   steamed rice or paratha

INGREDIENTS

500 gm medium-sized potatoes

3–4 green cardamom pods

2 large black cardamom pods

1 tbsp cumin seeds (*jeera*)

4–5 cloves

2 two-inch cinnamon sticks

2–3 bay leaves

1 tbsp black pepper powder

1 tbsp coriander powder

1 tbsp red chilli powder

½ tsp dry ginger powder

1 tbsp fennel powder

1 tbsp ghee

4 tbsp mustard oil (plus 1 cup more for frying)

Salt to taste

3½ cups water

1 tbsp coriander leaves, chopped

METHOD

Boil potatoes, peel and prick them with a toothpick. In a deep pan, pour mustard oil. Heat the oil and fry the potatoes.

In another pan, heat four tbsp of oil. Temper with cumin seeds, pepper powder, cloves, green and black cardamom pods, cinnamon sticks and bay leaves. When the cumin seeds start popping, add chilli powder and half a cup of water and stir. Now add in the dry ginger powder, fennel powder and coriander powder. Stir for another two minutes. Mix in the ghee and continue to stir gently.

Allow the ghee to rise to the top and then pour three cups of water. When the water begins to boil, add in the fried potatoes. Sprinkle salt over the dish, cover the pan and cook for 20 minutes on low heat, or until the gravy is reduced to a quarter of its original quantity.

Garnish with coriander leaves and serve hot.

MADRAS ONION SAMBAR

It is well-known that onions can bring tears to your eyes. In India, they can also bring governments down. Even a small rise in its price opens a floodgate of tears. The Madras onion is a miniature onion, and is commonly used in southern Indian cooking. Legend has it that the Sambar as a dish, originated from a blunder in the kitchens of the Tanjore Maratha ruler Shahu, where the cook was trying to make a Maharashtrian Amti Dal. Moong beans were used instead of the usual pigeon peas, and tamarind pulp instead of kokum as the souring agent. The result was relished and named after the guest that day, the second emperor of the Maratha empire, Sambhaji. Hence, Sambar.

RECIPE

 20–25 mins   Serves 4   steamed rice, dosa or idli

INGREDIENTS

½ cup yellow split pigeon peas (tur dal)

10–12 Madras onions (small shallots), peeled

¼ cup tomato, chopped

2 tbsp fresh coconut

A small ball of tamarind

2 green chillies

3 red chillies

2 tbsp coriander powder

½ tsp turmeric powder

½ tsp asafoetida

15–20 curry leaves

½ cup coriander leaves, chopped

½ tsp brown mustard seeds

½ tsp fenugreek seeds

1 tsp jaggery/sugar (optional)

2 tsp oil

Salt to taste

Water as required

METHOD

Soak tamarind in ¼ cup of warm water. Keep aside. Add tomato, turmeric and tur dal with 1½ cups of water in a pressure cooker. Cook for three whistles. Dry roast coconut in a pan till golden-brown. Dry roast red chillies, fenugreek seeds and coriander seeds separately. Heat one tsp of oil in a pan. Finely chop one of the Madras shallots and fry with the green chillies and half the curry leaves till translucent.

Grind all dry-roasted ingredients with shallot mixture in a mixer. Turn it into a smooth paste with two tbsp of water. Heat oil in a pan and add fenugreek and mustard seeds. When they splutter, stir in asafoetida and remaining curry leaves. Add peeled shallots and cook for 3–4 minutes. Squeeze the pulp out of the soaked tamarind and pour it in. Add salt and the ground paste and cook for a couple of minutes. Mix in the cooked dal and bring it to a boil. Cook till shallots are done. Add jaggery for a bolder flavour. Garnish with chopped coriander.

DOUBLE BEAN SUKKA

I'm not sure what double bean actually is. At home, where this recipe comes from, and in Marathi, we just call it, "double bee". I've never known an Indian name for this bean, though in English it is known as broad bean, lima bean or fava bean. The beans, once shelled (or you can buy the dehydrated version), are flat, plump and pretty to look at. However, once cooked, they lose their colour, but taste superb. They turn soft and buttery and absorb masalas really well. Like most beans, they are packed with minerals and full of protein and dietary fibre. Even now, in our genetically-modified-foods generation, these beans are available mainly during the winter.

RECIPE

 60 mins

 Serves 4

 steamed rice, chapati or dosa

INGREDIENTS

1 cup double beans (broad beans)

1 cup grated coconut

1 tsp garlic, crushed

1 tsp mustard seeds

½ tsp cumin seeds

¼ tsp split white lentils (urad dal)

1 sprig curry leaves

½ tsp red chilli powder

¼ tsp turmeric powder

1 tbsp oil

1 tsp salt to taste

2 cups water

METHOD

Soak the double beans in two cups of water overnight or at least for six hours.

Pressure cook the soaked beans with salt for two whistles. After the second whistle, cook for ten minutes on a medium flame. Then take the cooker off the flame and let the beans cool.

In the meantime, mix together thoroughly the grated coconut, garlic, red chilli powder and turmeric powder and set aside.

In a wide pan, heat oil and add the mustard seeds. When they begin to crackle, add cumin seeds and split white lentils. Fry for a minute or two. Throw in the curry leaves and stir for another two minutes.

Now add the boiled double beans and coconut mixture. Cook with a closed lid on medium heat for 10–12 minutes. Allow the dish to cook well, till the water completely dries up.

CHANE KA PULAO

As a vegetarian, how often have you been short-changed when it comes to biryani or *pulao*? This is one recipe that will help you avenge the times your options were limited to a vegetable pulao. Chane Ka *Pulao* is a great option. You can make it either with chickpeas (*kabuli* chana) or black chana, it's up to you. Personally, I like it with the latter, but I've given the *kabuli* chana variation, because most people treat black chana as poor man's food. Instead of relying on this preconceived notion, let us trust the judgement of our taste buds!

RECIPE

 30 mins   Serves 4–5   onion rings, lemon juice and raita

INGREDIENTS

3 cups Basmati rice, soaked for 30 mins

400 gm chickpeas, soaked overnight

1 medium onion, thinly sliced

3 black cardamom pods

2 one-inch cinnamon sticks

5–6 cloves

3 tsp cumin seeds (jeera)

1½ cup thick plain yoghurt

1 tsp ginger-garlic paste

3 tsp aniseed powder

2 tsp red chilli powder

1 tsp garam masala

4 tbsp oil

3 tsp salt

3½ cups water

METHOD

In a pan, heat oil. Add onion and fry till golden-brown. Add cardamom pods, cloves, cinnamon sticks and cumin seeds and stir-fry for about ten seconds. Now mix in the ginger-garlic paste, two tsp salt and red chilli powder. Sauté on medium heat for five minutes.

Once the dry spices are combined, pour in the curd and chickpeas. Mix well and cook on a medium-high flame till all the excess water evaporates. Add garam masala and aniseed powder to the dish. Cover with lid and cook on medium heat till the chickpeas are soft.

Finally, add salt, rice and enough water for the rice to cook. Cook on a high flame for seven minutes till the excess water dries up.

Now cover the pan. The lid should be tightly closed making sure no steam is let out. Cook on low heat for 15 minutes or till the rice is done.

PAKISTANI DAL TADKA

The Punjabi *mah ki* dal or black dal is what everyone drools over. Accepted that making good black dal requires painstaking care, but if well made, it is rich, creamy, buttery and well worth the effort. I have to argue, however, on behalf of the humble yellow Dal Tadka or Dal Fry. To my mind, just for pure flavour, nothing beats yellow dal tempered with

spices, green chillies and onion. Like nothing beats yellow Mori Dal that the Parsis make with rice and prawn patio; or a yellow Varan that the Maharashtrians make with rice and ghee. In Pakistan, Dal Tadka is made with urad dal (split white lentils) instead of tur dal (split pigeon peas) or *masur* dal (red lentils). This variant of Dal Tadka will leave you asking for more.

RECIPE

 45 mins   Serves 4   parathas or steamed rice and pickle

INGREDIENTS

1 cup split white lentils (urad dal)
½ tomato, finely chopped
½ tsp turmeric powder
½ tsp red chilli powder
Salt to taste
2 cups water

Tempering
½ red onion, thinly sliced
4–5 small round red chillies
1 tsp cumin seeds (*jeera*)
2 sprigs curry leaves
3 tbsp oil

Garnish
Coriander leaves, chopped
5 mint leaves, chopped
2 two-inch pieces of ginger, julienned
1 green chilli, julienned

METHOD

In a medium-sized saucepan, pour water to boil. When the water is boiling, add the urad dal, salt, turmeric powder, red chilli powder and tomato. Lower the heat to medium and cook for about 20 minutes, or until the water has evaporated. Lightly mash the dal with your fingers ensuring that the grains still remain whole.

In a frying pan, heat oil on medium flame. Add the onion and sauté for three minutes. Now add the cumin seeds, curry leaves, whole dried red chillies and fry until the onions turn golden-brown. Once the onions are golden-brown, pour the tempering over the dal. Mix gently.

Garnish with the ginger, coriander leaves, mint leaves, and green chilli.

Serve warm.

SOOKHA VATANA

This Sookha Vatana (green peas) recipe is one of my grandmom's favourites. With no disrespect to her or this recipe, I have to admit that I can eat green peas any which way: boiled, curried or even raw. But please don't try that, unless you have a cast iron stomach like mine.

Speaking fondly of the green pea itself, I need to explore a myth. The green pea is not a vegetable. In reality, each pea pod is a fruit, and the peas themselves are the seeds. Peas have been around for a staggeringly long time. The earliest evidence of their consumption dates back to almost 12,000 years.

RECIPE

 20 mins   Serves 4   chapati or puri

INGREDIENTS

4 cups green peas

1 tbsp ginger, grated

1 tsp cumin seeds (*jeera*)

2 tbsp coriander powder

1 pinch asafoetida

1 tbsp dry mango powder (*amchur*)

1 tsp turmeric powder

1 tbsp garam masala

½ tsp red chilli powder

1 cup fresh coriander leaves

1 tbsp vegetable oil or olive oil

Salt to taste

Water as required

METHOD

Heat oil in a pan and add asafoetida, cumin seeds and grated ginger. When the cumin seeds begin to crackle, add the green peas, coriander powder, red chilli powder, garam masala and dry mango powder. Stir continuously for the spices to combine. Add enough water to cover the peas in the pan. Cover with a lid and cook for five minutes, till the green peas are soft.

Remove the lid. Add half the coriander leaves and salt. Stir well.

Garnish with coriander leaves and serve warm.

Breaking bread
over a Kolhapuri
lunch with culinary
expert Karen Anand
at Opal Hotel,
Kolhapur,
Maharashta

AKKI ROTI

Karnataka, the land of Udipi Cuisine. If Udipi is in Karnataka, so is Coorg and Mangalore, and the food from each region is distinctive. The cusine is influenced by Karnataka's three South Indian neighbours, as well as the state of Maharashtra.

From coastal Mangalore, Karwar to the hilly climate of Coorg, Chikmangalur to Bijapur, Gulbarga, to the Kodavas with the influence of Kerala, the state has it all. From this state comes the Akki Roti. It is a rice-based breakfast dish, very similar to dosa. I love it for its soft and crisp texture. Above all, I love that it allows you the freedom to add and subtract flavours and tastes in order to customize it to your whims.

RECIPE

 40 mins   Serves 2   plain yoghurt or chutney

INGREDIENTS

½ cup green gram (*moong* dal)

½ cup fresh coconut, shredded

2 cups white rice flour

¼ cup carrot, shredded

2½ green chillies, finely chopped

1 tsp cumin seeds (*jeera*)

¼ tsp asafoetida powder

½ cup vegetable oil

Salt to taste

1 cup water

2 tbsp coriander leaves, finely chopped

METHOD

Soak the *moong* beans and refrigerate overnight. Drain the beans and reserve the excess water. In a bowl, combine the soaked beans, rice flour, cumin seeds, green chillies, asafoetida, coriander leaves, coconut, shredded carrot and salt. Gradually add water, kneading well with your hands to form a workable dough.

Shape the dough into balls (about the size of a table-tennis ball). Flatten one ball of dough into a thin, round roti using a rolling pin.

Heat two tbsp of vegetable oil in a griddle or skillet over medium heat. Place the roti and fry until golden-brown, for about 30–40 seconds. Flip the roti over and fry until golden. Repeat the process for each roti.

Serve hot.

BHOPALI ROTI

Whether it is a hot baguette, a freshly baked Brun Pav or a soft and buttered Tandoori Naan, I have always been a sucker for great bread. Fresh, white bread evidently sends my sugar levels shooting through the roof. Still, I cannot resist the aromas that roll out from a bakery making fresh *sheermals*, *roomalis*, *baqarkhanis* or just plain chapati or paratha. The Bhopali Roti is one of the tastiest. As its name suggests, it originates from the *nawabi* state of Bhopal.

Historically, as in Hyderabad and Lucknow, there has been a lot of grandstanding in Bhopal about the virtuosity of and indulgence towards its homegrown cuisine. This roti is one of the finest examples of the gastronomical delights of that princely state.

RECIPE

 30 mins   Serves 4–5   green chutney or pickle

INGREDIENTS

1½ cup whole wheat flour (atta)

½ cup rice flour

3 green chillies, chopped

3 tbsp cashews, ground

3 tbsp coriander powder

1 tsp cumin seeds, dry roasted and ground

6 saffron strands soaked in 2 tbsp warm milk

2 tbsp ghee

1 tsp salt

Water for kneading dough

½ cup fresh coriander leaves, finely chopped

Additional ghee for frying

METHOD

Sift in and mix together the atta, rice flour and salt in bowl. Rub in two tbsp of ghee. Add the remaining ingredients to the dough, except the ghee for frying. Gently pour water and knead the dough just as you would to make a chapati.

Apply your hands lightly to make a soft dough. When the dough is ready, shape the it into ten small balls. On a flat surface, sprinkle some flour. On this floured surface, roll out each ball into medium-sized rotis.

On a hot griddle or tava, gently place the rolled out dough and roast. As the roti browns, smear a little ghee and drizzle some around the edges. Cook the roti until both sides are golden-brown.

Serve hot.

VARIAS

Varias, or Orias as they are sometimes called, is just one more in the medley of breads made by Mumbai's East Indian community. Be it the new year, a wedding or a christening, no meal is complete without this dish. The Varia is closer to a Medu Vada than a Sanna (steamed savoury rice balls), because, not only is it deep-fried like a Medu Wada, it is also made with heavier flours, such as whole wheat and urad dal. Therefore, it's best to prepare the batter the previous night, so that it has enough time to rise. The Varia is then shaped into little balls with holes in the centre, much like the Medu Vada, and then deep-fried till golden. But like many East Indian breads, it is sweetened. So to me, it is more of a doughnut than a Medu Vada.

RECIPE

 20 mins   Serves 4   curry

INGREDIENTS

500 gm white lentil (urad dal) flour

500 gm refined wheat flour (maida)

500 gm rice flour

100 gm sugar

2 tsp yeast or toddy

Salt to taste

Oil for deep-frying

METHOD

In a bowl, knead the maida with the urad dal flour, rice flour, sugar and salt. Now mix in the yeast. Knead the dough so that it is thick but light enough to form doughnuts. Leave it overnight to rise well.

Make rings out of the mixture with holes in the centre, like doughnuts.

In a wok or a deep pan, add enough oil for deep-frying. Once the oil starts bubbling, put the doughnuts in and fry them until brown.

Remove the fried Varias with a perforated ladle and place them on absorbent paper or tissue that will help remove the excess oil.

ALOO PARATHA TADKEWALA

Feeding someone an Aloo Paratha is like smothering him with love and asphyxiating him with an overdose of complex carbs. But find me a man who can resist one and I will give up eating cabbage. From truckers on National Highway 1 to the aristocratic Talwars and Dhariwals, those traversing Punjab's highways and eateries have stopped for an Aloo Paratha at least once in their lives. Unfortunately, most of them roast the paratha in a tandoor and not on a *tava*. Therein lies the difference between taste and chaste – the purity of any stuffed paratha depends on the tava. Still, if you want to play around with the Aloo Paratha sanctity, try adding a *tadka* like I do.

RECIPE

30 mins   Serves 4–5   white butter, green chutney or pickle

INGREDIENTS

The Stuffing
3–4 potatoes, boiled and mashed
1 onion, sliced
2 tsp red chilli powder
1 tsp garam masala
2 tsp coriander-cumin powder
½ tsp dry mango powder
Fresh coriander, finely chopped
Bread crumbs

Tempering
1 tbsp oil
1 tsp mustard seeds
1 tsp fenugreek seeds
1 sprig curry leaves

The Parathas
2 cups whole wheat flour (atta)
3 tbsp plain yoghurt
Oil or ghee for making parathas
Water for kneading dough

METHOD

Heat oil in a pan and add the fenugreek seeds, mustard seeds and curry leaves. Add onion and fry till golden, then add the potatoes, red chilli powder, garam masala, coriander-cumin powder, dry mango powder and finely chopped coriander. Stir vigorously till the spices are cooked and mixed into the potatoes and onion.

In a bowl, knead together the flour and curd, pouring water in as required. There should be enough dough for ten small balls. Roll out each ball into medium-sized parathas. Place the stuffing in the centre of the paratha and seal it by lifting the edges and folding them towards the centre. Use a rolling pin to flatten it out a little. While rolling the paratha, grease the surface either with oil or flour to prevent it from sticking.

Heat a tava and cook the paratha on it till it browns. Then smear some oil or ghee around the edges and flip to cook the other side. Roast the paratha until both sides are golden-brown.

In the kitchens of Jafferbhai Mansuri, Mumbai, frying up the masala for Mughlai Kheema

HINGATELACHE VATANE

I have memories of all the ladies in the house shelling green peas. One by one, they would pry open the shells, diligently looking for worms that hid behind the peas to avoid discovery. Therefore, the advent of frozen peas was a blessing. Green peas are also one of those rare preserved vegetables that actually taste good when cooked. To maintain my peace of mind, I avoid reading the information supplied on the pack to keep unpalatable revelations at bay. Being frozen doesn't change their flavour and that's what really matters.

Hingatelache Vatane was the first dish that I learned to cook when I moved out of my parents' home. It barely takes any time at all to cook green peas with asafoetida in oil.

RECIPE

15 mins   Serves 4   chapati

INGREDIENTS

The Kitchen King Masala

1 tbsp grated coconut

2 tsp fresh coriander, chopped

1 tsp coriander-cumin seeds powder

½ tsp red chilli powder

½ tsp sugar

The Main Dish

2 cups green peas

2 tbsp oil

½ tsp mustard seeds

¼ tsp asafoetida

¼ tsp turmeric powder

½ tsp red chilli powder

1 tsp Kitchen King Masala

½ cup water

Salt to taste

METHOD

Simply mix together all the ingredients

listed (the chopped coriander, grated coconut, coriander-cumin seeds powder, red chilli powder and sugar). Keep aside.

In a wok, heat oil and add the mustard seeds. Let the seeds splutter and crackle. Then add asafoetida and sauté for a few seconds. Add the green peas, turmeric powder, red chilli powder, Kitchen King Masala and salt. Pour half a cup of water and stir well. Cook on a low flame until the green peas are soft and all the water has evaporated.

Serve hot.

GOAN POTATO CURRY

When you think of Goan food, you are most likely to consider the Vindaloo and Sorpatel and fish curry. But the Hindu cuisine in Goa is a treasure trove of enlightenment. Yes, coconut is ever-present even in these dishes. But as the Goan Hindu can be fairly austere and traditional, there is a huge, lip-smacking variety of vegetarian food suited to scriptural practices. I remember my first-ever meal at the Mandovi Hotel in Panjim. The spread included Tondak (a dish of beans and cashew nuts), Solachi Kadi (coconut and kokum curry), Khatkhate (mixed vegetable stew), Vangyache Kaap (panfried brinjal) and Cashew and Tender Coconut Sukke. Below is another favourite vegetarian dish from Goa – a delectable potato curry.

RECIPE

 45 mins   Serves 4   goan red rice (*ukade* rice)

INGREDIENTS

1 large coconut, grated (for the milk)
2 additional tbsp grated coconut
2 green chillies
2 red chillies
4 garlic cloves
2 onions, chopped
2 tomatoes, blanched and pureed
1 large boiled potato, peeled
1 capsicum, diced
1 cup mixed vegetables, boiled
1 tbsp fresh coriander, finely chopped
½ cup fresh cream
6 cashew nuts
1 one-inch cinnamon stick
2 cloves
1 bay leaf
3 peppercorns
½ tsp cumin seeds
½ tsp mustards seeds
2 tbsp oil or ghee
Salt to taste
2 cups of water

METHOD

Blend the large coconut's flesh with two cups of water to form a thick paste. Strain coconut mixture to get thick coconut milk. Keep aside.

Dry roast cinnamon, pepper, cloves, bay leaf and cumin. Grind to a fine powder. Keep aside. In a pan, add a tsp of ghee and mix onions and two tbsp of grated coconut. Fry onions till tender and translucent and grated coconut till golden-brown. Grind together tomatoes, red chillies, garlic, fried coconut and half the fried onions to a paste. Grind cashew nuts to a fine powder and keep aside.

Heat remaining ghee and fry potato chunks till golden. Drain and keep aside. Fry capsicums, drain and keep aside. Add mustard seeds to the ghee. Let it splutter. Add mixed vegetables. Stir for a minute. Mix in the ground spices. Add remaining fried onions, ground paste, cashew powder, coconut milk and stir till it comes to a boil. Simmer till thickened. Stir in fresh cream. Garnish with coriander and whole cashews.

PAKORA DAHI KADHI

I cannot fathom how a state with a never-ending coastline and an almost endless supply of seafood can be so staunchly vegetarian. Geography has nearly always dictated food habits in most parts of the country, but Gujarat remains happily deviant thanks to the strong influence of Jainism, as well as Vaishnavism.

But in most other ways, the state quails to nature and its very dry climate. The aridness of Gujarat encourages the cultivation of wheat, maize and bajra (pearl millet), instead of rice. Hence rotlis, chapatis and bhakris form the daily fare and are accompanied by side dishes that suit this feast of unleavened bread. Dahi Kadhi, for instance, is a vegetarian's delight and as Gujarati as it can get.

Gujarati food is also influenced by its neighbour, Maharashtra, and dishes from the southern part of the state can be quite spicy, as opposed to the sweet flavour traditionally associated with this cuisine. But in Gujarat, a meal is never complete without kadhi, dal, roti and shaak. Here is a taste of the spicy side of Gujarat.

RECIPE

 60 mins   Serves 4   steamed rice and pickle

INGREDIENTS

The Pakoras

1 green chilli or jalapeno, chopped

¼ tsp red chilli powder or cayenne pepper

2 tsp onions, chopped

½ tsp ginger, grated

1 cup gram flour (besan)

1 pinch cumin seeds (jeera)

½ tsp fennel seeds (optional)

1 pinch turmeric powder

¼ tsp garam masala

2–3 cups oil for frying

Water for mixing the batter

METHOD

In a bowl, mix together the gram flour, chopped onion, green chilli, grated ginger, garam masala, red chilli powder, turmeric powder, cumin seeds, fennel seeds and salt.

Pour just enough water to make a thick batter. In a deep-frying pan, heat the oil. Drop the batter in the form of small balls into the hot oil. Fry the pakoras until they turn crisp and golden. Remove from the pan and place on paper towels to drain the excess oil.

Keep the pakoras warm in an oven on low heat.

In a blender, mix the curd, water, turmeric powder, salt, red chilli powder and gram flour. Blend the mixture until it has the consistency and appearance of buttermilk. Keep aside for

The Curd Base

2 cups thick curd

4 cups water

1 pinch turmeric powder

1 pinch salt

1 pinch red chilli powder

1 tbsp gram flour (besan)

The Kadhi

1 large tomato, chopped

1 large onion, sliced long

2–3 garlic cloves, minced

4–5 dried red chillies

2 tsp mustard seeds

1 tsp cumin seeds (jeera)

1 tsp coriander seeds

½ tsp fenugreek seeds

7–8 curry leaves

2–3 cloves

1 tsp ginger paste

1–2 tsp tamarind paste (mixed with 1 tbsp water)

1 tsp turmeric powder

3 tsp garam masala

1 tsp red chilli powder

1 tsp fenugreek leaves/powder

2 tbsp mustard oil or ghee

Salt to taste

2 tbsp coriander leaves, chopped

30 minutes.

Pour mustard oil in a wok and heat it until it begins to smoke. Add in the mustard, fenugreek, cumin and coriander seeds, as well as the cloves. Let them all crackle and pop. Then add curry leaves and dry red chillies to the mixture.

Add the slivers of onion and fry until they turn golden-brown. Then mix in the garlic and ginger. Sauté for three minutes, making sure the mixture does not stick to the bottom of the pan. Add in the chopped tomato and fry for another 3–4 minutes.

In a fresh pan, heat oil. Pour in the tamarind paste and cook it for 4–5 minutes. Add turmeric powder, garam masala, red chilli powder and salt. Fry until the oil starts floating on the top, giving it a dark reddish-brown colour.

Now add the fried onion and tomato mixture to this. Gently stir the curry on medium heat. Bring it to a boil, let it simmer and cook for 3–5 minutes. Now cook the curry on low flame for 20 minutes, stirring occasionally. Stir for another five minutes and check if it's thick enough and looks dark yellow. Stir for five more minutes and then sprinkle it with dry fenugreek leaves.

Let it boil for another two minutes. Now add the pakoras to the kadhi. Boil and stir gently for about three minutes.

Garnish with coriander leaves. Serve hot.

CHARCHARLELI BATATI

Charcharleli means crusty, and *batati* is potato. I inherited my grandmom's recipes from my aunt Suhas Velkar, written in neat Roman script by my grandad. My aunt is one of the finest cooks I have ever come across, second only to her mother – my grandmom, Leeli. Of all her recipes, this one needs special mention. It's a simple dish made with potato, oil and masala, but needs exceptional finesse for it to turn out right.

My aunt would make it at the drop of a hat, whether I dropped in for lunch unannounced or we were picnicking at her house in Matheran. The secret is in that one ingredient that makes all food taste great – lots of oil.

RECIPE

 20 mins   Serves 4   hot chapati or poori

INGREDIENTS

2 cups potatoes, sliced

3 tbsp oil

½ tsp mustard seeds

¼ tsp asafoetida

1 tsp red chilli powder

¼ tsp turmeric powder

Salt to taste

Coriander leaves, chopped

METHOD

Heat oil in a wok and add the mustard seeds. Let the seeds splutter and crackle. Then add asafoetida and sauté for a few seconds. Add sliced potatoes and mix well. Stir in the red chilli powder, turmeric powder and salt. Cook this for a few minutes till the aromas are released. Cover the potatoes with a lid and let them cook. Pour water on the lid to prevent the curry from burning and sticking to the pan. Stir occasionally.

Once the potatoes are cooked, transfer the contents to a serving dish and sprinkle freshly chopped coriander leaves on top.

Serve hot.

EGG

Egg is no longer just a breakfast food. You'll find it in burgers, baked atop casseroles, poached on pasta, in a curry, as a pizza topping, scrambled with masala and in desserts. With eggs you can fry, poach, bake and cook. You can even leaven, bind, thicken, coat, glaze, clarify, moisturize. They submissively perform uncounted and untold culinary functions. Egg is that magic additive that gives a soufflé its fluff, a sponge it's lightness and makes a meringue float. It is also the first choice of those vegetarians taking Montessori steps towards carnivorism.

AKOORI ON TOAST

Masala scrambled eggs, Parsi style – that's what Akoori is essentially. I blame 79 of my 97 kilos on my Parsi friends and their food. Had it not been for their enticing cuisine, I might have been a slim, trim 50 kilos. But every ounce of my generous pounds pays homage to their native hospitality and expertise in the kitchen. My earliest memories of extravagant, decadent breakfasts start with the old Fountain Hotel, Mahabaleshwar (before the Parsi owners sold out). Those spectacular breakfasts can still be had at Il Palazzo, Panchgani.

Dhansak powder, often used in Parsi cooking, is a variation of sambar masala, combining whole spices, roasted and ground to a fine powder. It is readily available at most masala stores.

RECIPE

 15 mins   Serves 2 buttered toast

INGREDIENTS

6 large eggs

25 gm butter

½ cup cream

2 small spring onions, finely chopped

1 green chilli, de-seeded and chopped

½ tsp garlic, finely grated

½ tsp cumin seeds (*jeera*)

½ tsp turmeric powder

½ tsp dhansak powder

½ tsp red chilli powder

Salt to taste

Handful of coriander, chopped

METHOD

In a bowl, beat eggs with milk and a little salt. Set aside.

Heat a little butter in a frying pan, add onions and fry until almost golden-brown. Then add in the garlic, cumin seeds and green chilli and fry to release the aromas. To this mixture, add turmeric powder, *dhansak* powder and red chilli powder. Cook for one more minute.

Now pour in the egg mixture. Mix well and stir gently on medium heat. Cook till the dish reaches

a nice creamy consistency. Sprinkle it with fresh coriander leaves and the finely chopped spring onion and mix gently.

Toast some bread and butter generously. Serve the eggs on the buttered toast.

PIZZA SUNNY SIDE UP

Laugh at me if you will, but the first pizza I ever ate was at Haji Ali Juice Centre in Mumbai. That was before I traveled to Italy, New York or any other place that is known for its pizzas. There was no known pizza chain in Mumbai at the time and only the odd five-star hotel served this Italian bread.

Haji Ali Juice Centre made its pizza with a thick base, bottled tomato ketchup, piles of onions, capsicum and grated processed cheese. It is made the same way today, and the taste hasn't changed either. However spurious that may sound, the pizza tasted really good! It also helped me keep an open mind on what one could do with a so-called authentic recipe.

RECIPE

30 mins   Serves 2   rocket salad leaves

INGREDIENTS

The Pizza Dough

3½ cup refined wheat flour (maida)

2–3 eggs

2¼ tsp yeast

¼ cup olive oil

1 tbsp sugar

1 tsp salt

1 cup cold water

The Pizza Sauce

500 gm tomato puree

1 large garlic clove, crushed

1 tsp dried basil

1 tsp dried oregano

1 tbsp extra virgin olive oil

Salt to taste

Black pepper to taste

METHOD

Mix flour, yeast, oil, salt and sugar in a bowl. Add water slowly and gently knead the dough with your fingers till it separates from the side of the bowl. Cover with a damp cloth and let it rise until it doubles in size (2–3 hours).

Pour olive oil in a saucepan on low heat. When oil is hot, fry the garlic till it starts to colour (but do not let it turn brown). Stir in the tomato puree and cook on medium heat, adding basil and oregano. Cover the pan and cook the sauce on low heat for ten minutes. Mix in salt and pepper to taste.

Preheat the oven for 20 minutes at 180ºC. Make three balls out of the dough and roll them out. Make sure the pizza base is half a centimetre thick and the edges are turned up slightly, so the pizza sauce does not drip. Spread the sauce evenly. Break a couple of eggs on top of it. Bake at 190ºC for 15–20 minutes. Garnish with rocket salad leaves and a drizzle of olive oil.

INDIAN SCOTCH EGG CURRY

Scotch eggs are boiled eggs encased in minced mutton and then fried. It is quite similar to an Anday ka Kofta or a Nargisi Kofta. Whether the Scotch egg came first or the *kofta* did, is debatable. Exclusive London provisioner, Fortnum & Mason, claim they invented the Scotch egg in 1738. Not that it really matters to me. I am a big devotee of Egg Curry, and this one remarkably incorporates the Scotch egg.

RECIPE

 40 mins   Serves 4   rice or hot *pav*

INGREDIENTS

3 hard-boiled eggs

The Mince
500 gm minced mutton
1 egg for frying
1 small onion, chopped
4–5 green chillies, chopped
1 tsp gram, ground
1 tsp poppy seeds (*khus khus*), ground
1 tbsp ginger-garlic paste
1 tbsp garam masala
1 tsp red chilli powder
½ cup oil
Salt to taste
Small bunch of fresh coriander, chopped

The Gravy
4 onions, finely sliced
4 tbsp ginger-garlic paste
½ cup plain yoghurt
2 tsp red chilli powder
½ tsp turmeric powder
4 tbsp coriander powder
1 tbsp garam masala
½ tsp mace (*javitri*) powder
½ tsp nutmeg (*jaiphal*) powder
1 cup oil
Salt to taste

METHOD

Mix together all the ingredients of the mince. Divide this mixture into three equal parts. Coat the three boiled eggs with the mince mixture, giving it an oval shape. In a bowl, beat the raw egg and dip the mince-coated eggs into it. Heat oil in a pan and deep-fry the eggs. Take them out of the oil and then deep-freeze the eggs for 15 minutes. Then with a sharp knife, slit the eggs into two halves and keep aside.

Heat the oil and fry the onions in it till they turn golden-brown. Cool the onions and then grind them. In the oil, add ginger-garlic paste, red chilli powder, turmeric powder, coriander powder and salt. Cook until the raw smell fades away. Add plain yoghurt, nutmeg powder and mace powder. Cook till the gravy thickens. Add the eggs and cook on slow flame for five minutes.

Garnish with the tomato and green chillies and serve warm.

FUGIAS

Imagine the sharp, tangy and spicy gravy of an Indal (Vindaloo) with a soft, small pillow of sweetness. That's exactly what a Fugia is. It's Maharashtra's East Indian community's version of bread. Their cuisine is an engaging and luscious combination of Portuguese, Maharashtrian and coastal tastes. Surprisingly, the recipes and masalas used in their cooking go only as far back as the days of British India.

Like the Goans and the Syrian Christians from Kerala, whose mainstay is rice, the East Indians are rice and bread eaters. Though rice is included in a variety of preparations, no festival or marriage is complete without *wadds*, *polias*, *chatiaps*, *sannas* or my favourite, the *fugia*.

RECIPE

 15 mins   Serves 2 curry

INGREDIENTS

3 eggs

1 kg refined wheat flour (maida)

½ cup coconut milk

½ cup rice flour

1 tbsp dry yeast

Oil for frying

A pinch of salt

Sugar to taste

METHOD

Sift the maida into a large bowl. To this, add the coconut milk, sugar, salt and rice flour, and knead them all together well.

In a separate bowl, break and beat the eggs, and then add them to the flour mixture. Now knead in the yeast until the flour mixture turns thick, but is light enough to form balls. Leave the flour overnight to ferment and rise.

Roll the dough into small balls by grasping it with the left hand and squeezing it out through your thumb and forefinger.

In a wok or a deep pan, add enough oil for frying. When the oil becomes hot, drop the flour balls in.

Fry the *fugia* balls till they turn brown. Remove them from the oil with a perforated ladle and place them on paper towels to drain the excess oil.

Fugias are best served with curry.

GOAN EGG DROP CURRY

Egg Curry or Egg Masala is the safest dish to order in a cheap Indian restaurant; however, its preparation can vary. A Muslim restaurant will give it to you with the same curry used in Chicken Fry; a Malvani restaurant will make it in coconut curry; a Punjabi restaurant will do the onion-tomato version, but all these interpretations will undoubtedly serve the curry with hard-boiled eggs. There is a far more interesting way to make the Egg Curry – my mother makes a typical Pathare Prabhu (a Mumbai-based community I'm from) Andyache Bhujne. And the Parsis have made an art out of dropping fresh eggs into every dish! The recipe below is a Goan Egg Curry, which also drops in eggs, instead of boiling them.

RECIPE

 15 mins   Serves 2   rice

INGREDIENTS

4 eggs

6 Kashmiri red chillies

1 onion

1 tomato

½ cup thick coconut milk

4 tbsp grated coconut

2 tsp coriander seeds

1 tsp cumin seeds

2 garlic cloves

½ tsp turmeric powder

1 cup water

Small bunch of coriander leaves, chopped

2–3 green chillies, slit

Salt to taste

METHOD

Grind the spices (Kashmiri chillies, cumin and coriander seeds, turmeric powder and grated coconut) with water. Heat oil in a casserole and then add chopped onion and garlic. Add tomato and sauté till the onion turns golden-brown. Then add the ground masala and salt. Stir-fry for a few minutes.

Pour in a cup of water and allow the dish to cook for 4–5 mins. Then gently break the eggs over the gravy, so that the yolk does not break while dropping in. Once all the eggs are in, pour some hot curry on the eggs with a spoon. Allow the eggs to cook. Now pour in the coconut milk. Keep pouring the curry onto the eggs while cooking.

Once cooked, garnish with slit green chillies and chopped fresh green coriander. Your Goan Egg Drop Curry is ready.

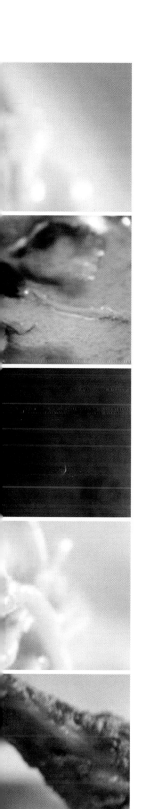

CHICKEN

Everyone likes chicken. Chicken is versatile, easy to cook, lower in saturated fat than most meats, has a high level of good protein and above all, is available everywhere. It has conquered all cuisines in India. Also, vegetarians often use chicken as a positive first step to enter the wonderful world of meat.

Personally, I find chicken meat tasteless, unless of course, you shove it into a tandoor or infuse it with spices and masalas. If you do this, the chicken then becomes the bearer of great taste.

ESPERANZA'S CHICKEN CURRY

In the early 50s and 60s of Bombay, even up to the 80s, most well-to-do non-Hindus would have a Pedrina, an Emrencia, a Magarida, an Aida or at least a Rosy in their homes, cooking up great feasts for meal times. My friends had an Esperanza. Her chicken curry was half Goan, half Chira Bazaar and wholly delectable. Although the curry was not authentically Goan, it left us greatly content and today, I remember it with a lingering sense of wistfulness. This, along with steaming platefuls of unpolished red rice is, as they say in Goa, *ukadem xitt!*

RECIPE

 30 mins   Serves 4   steamed rice or hot *pav*

INGREDIENTS

1 kg chicken

4 onions, finely sliced

3 garlic pods, crushed

1 tbsp ginger, chopped

3 tbsp roasted almonds, sliced

2 tsp cardamom

4 cloves

1 tbsp cinnamon powder

1 tsp black pepper powder

1 tsp red chilli powder

¼ tsp saffron

2 cups thick coconut milk

2 cups plain yoghurt

2 tbsp oil

1 tsp salt

METHOD

Heat oil in a pan and add in the onions, cinnamon, cardamom, black pepper and cloves. Fry the onions and spices till they turn golden-brown. Then add in the chopped ginger and garlic. Fry them also until golden-brown. Add the chicken and cook till the chicken changes colour.

After the colour of the chicken changes, mix in the red chilli powder, yoghurt, salt and saffron. Mix well by stirring continuously. Cook till the chicken is tender, pouring in a little water if required.

Once the chicken is tender, pour coconut milk over it and add in the almonds. Cook for another five minutes and allow the sauce to reduce. Do not overcook, as coconut milk tends to curdle.

Serve hot.

KAJU CHICKEN KORMA

As far as I know, Korma is an imperative. If you know how to make a good Korma, you can make almost any Mughlai food. My Muslim friends insist that Korma is the basis for many recipes, including the Yakhni (a yoghurt and saffron-based meat broth). Korma is basically braised mutton, stewed in spices, fried onions and beaten curd. It's a dish often reserved for special occasions, just like biryani. However, nowadays, Korma is mostly made on weekends in well-heeled Muslim homes in Hyderabad, Lucknow and Agra, where adding rich nuts, like cashews goes without saying. The cashew paste adds a silky richness to the Korma. Making it with chicken adds a feather to your cap of health.

RECIPE

40 mins   Serves 2   or roti, chapati or hot bread

INGREDIENTS

500 gm chicken

2 medium-sized onions, thinly chopped

½ cup plain yoghurt, beaten

½ cup cashew paste

¼ cup fresh cream

2 tsp ginger, sliced

½ cup grated coconut

3–4 green chillies

2 garlic cloves

3–4 green cardamoms

2 tbsp poppy seeds (*khus khus*)

¼ cup oil

1 tsp salt

METHOD

In a mixer, add poppy seeds, grated coconut, garlic, green cardamom, salt and green chillies. Grind the ingredients to a paste, pouring a little water.

Heat oil in a pan and stir-fry the thinly chopped onions until they become translucent.

Add the chopped ginger and chicken and fry with the onions. Before the colour of the chicken starts to change, add the beaten yoghurt and cashew paste. Cook for 2–3 minutes. Now, add the ground paste to the chicken and mix it well.

Cover the chicken and cook till it is tender and all the spices have cooked and blended well. Once the chicken is done, add fresh cream and cook for another 2–3 minutes.

Serve hot.

Get your ducks in a row. With my cousin, Rahul Velkar, a restauranteur, at China Town, Soho, London

CHICKEN PASTA CURRY

I say, why not? After all, we Indians do love spicy, oily preparations. If we can expertly mangle a Chinese dish to make it our own, then why can we not do the same with spaghetti? Pasta may be synonymous with Italian food, but how did it find itself in Italy? Marco Polo, the great Venetian traveller, allegedly brought it to Italy from China in the 13th century. He called it Macaroni. And what is pasta, if not the cousin of a noodle? So, let's add a little besan, masalas and curry leaves to spaghetti and make it our own.

RECIPE

15 mins   Serves 3   mango pickle or chutney

INGREDIENTS

500 gm boneless bhicken, de-skinned and cubed

¼ cup gram flour (*besan*)

4 red bell peppers, diced and de-seeded

3–4 fresh curry leaves

1 tbsp ginger–garlic paste

1 tsp turmeric powder

2 tsp red chilli powder or hot paprika

¼ cup water

1 cup coconut milk

3 green chillies, thinly sliced

½ cup coriander leaves, finely chopped

1 lemon, thinly sliced

250 gm packet spaghetti

Salt to taste

Water for cooking

METHOD

In a small skillet over medium heat, cook the gram flour by stirring frequently until it darkens slightly (about five minutes). Transfer the toasted flour into a bowl to cool.

On medium high heat, cook red bell peppers and curry leaves for two minutes, stirring constantly. Add cubed chicken and cook until no longer pink. Add ginger-garlic paste and fry.

Mix turmeric and red chilli powders with the gram flour. Sprinkle the spice mixture over the chicken. Cook for another two minutes. Pour ¼ cup of water to prevent the spices from sticking to the pan's bottom. Pour coconut milk, mix with the chicken and cook on low flame.

Add salt to taste to a large pot of water and bring it to a boil. Add the spaghetti and cook uncovered, stirring occasionally until cooked through, but still firm to the bite. Drain excess water and refresh the spaghetti under cold water, so that it does not become lumpy.

Transfer the hot spaghetti to a serving bowl. Pour the chicken mixture over it and garnish with sliced green chillies and cilantro leaves.

KORI CHICKEN SUKKA

A small village called Katapady near Udupi. The backwaters of the Udyavara river flowing through lush paddy fields. A settlement of alluvial huts separated by grassy fences. A young lady drying rotis in the afternoon sun. I was about to make my greatest discovery. Chicken, as I have often said, is not my choice of meat, but a robustly flavoured dry coconut curry called Kori Chicken Sukka changed my mind. And that's what the young lady drying rotis cooked for me in an earthen pot on a wood fire.

Kori Roti, also known as Kori Ghashi, is a Mangalorean comfort food. The curry itself is dry (*sukka*), mildly and delicately spiced and its smooth texture delightfully intruded upon by coarse coconut.

RECIPE

40 mins   Serves 4   mangalorean roti or *pav*

INGREDIENTS

1 kg chicken

2 cups onion, sliced

12 garlic cloves

30 roasted Kashmiri red chillies

½-inch ball of tamarind

1½ cup coconut

1-inch cinnamon stick

3–4 cloves

½ tsp turmeric powder

2 tbsp roasted coriander seeds

2 tsp roasted cumin seeds

1 tsp roasted peppercorns

1 tsp roasted fenugreek seeds

½ tsp poppy seeds (*khus-khus*)

Salt to taste

METHOD

Heat a shallow pan on medium heat and add oil. Add poppy seeds, cloves and cinnamon and stir for a few seconds. Add half a cup of sliced onions. Fry for a minute or so. Add turmeric and six garlic cloves. Fry till onions are soft. Add the rest of the spices, including coriander seeds, one tsp cumin seeds, peppercorns and fenugreek. Frying till you smell their aroma. Add red chillies and tamarind and fry for a minute. When this cools, grind onions, red chilli and spice mixture into a fine paste.

In another large vessel, rub half this masala paste into the chicken. Place pan on medium heat. Add the rest of the onions and salt and mix well. Cover the pan and cook on medium heat till the chicken is tender and cooked.

On an iron pan, roast coconut with the rest of the cumin seeds and six garlic cloves for two minutes. Cool the mixture and coarse grind it. Add this to the cooked chicken with half a cup of water. Cover and cook for 8 to 10 minutes.

BOMBAY CHICKEN CURRY

Any old English pub in London will serve you a curry in its uniquely misunderstood style. The curry migrated to the UK with nostalgic sahibs returning to their homeland. It became a rage in the late 19th century, relished by those who had robust Victorian appetites. Curry powder became available off the shelf and a brand called Selim's Curry Paste even advertised it as 'highly digestive, anti-bilious, anti-spasmodic, anti-flatulent, soothing and invigorating to the stomach and bowels'. Today, there are over 9,000 curry houses in the UK. The British version is saucy, creamy, sweet and often bereft of coconut. The recipe below is a real curry with coconut. It is also an adaptation attributed to Mumbai's mixed culture, spontaneity and wonderful recklessness.

RECIPE

 60 mins   Serves 8   steamed rice or hot *pav*

INGREDIENTS

2 kg chicken

125 gm desiccated coconut

4 garlic pods, crushed

2 tbsp olive oil

½ tsp turmeric powder

1 tsp red chilli powder

½ tsp black pepper powder

10 curry leaves

2 tbsp white vinegar

2 tbsp olive oil

1 tbsp sugar

METHOD

Clean, de-skin, wash and cut the chicken into two-inch pieces.

Place the chicken in a pan, cover with water and bring to a boil. Cover with a lid and slow-cook the chicken for about 30 minutes or until the chicken

is tender.

Once the chicken is cooked, drain the stock and keep aside. In another pan, heat oil and add vinegar, coconut, garlic, cumin seeds, turmeric, chilli, pepper, ginger and curry leaves. Sauté the whole for about 2–3 minutes.

Add the chicken pieces, reserved stock and sugar. Bring to a boil and then cook on low flame. Let it simmer for 15 minutes till the curry thickens.

Serve hot.

GOMES CAFREAL

"From serving in the city's cafes and eating-places, Goans moved to join newly formed steamship companies and sailed the high seas as cooks, butlers and stewards. Here they perfected their skills mastering the art of confectionery and pastry-making, particularly under Italian professionals. The more venturesome utilised this expertise to set up independent cake-shops and restaurants in Bombay and other cities" (Albuquerque, 2014). In Post-British Mumbai, those who had any standing in society boasted of a Goan cook or butler, such as an Eddie or Gomes, who'd whisk up fine soufflés, au gratins and potages. Then, there was also the legendary Miguel Arcanjo Mascarenhas or "Masci", who ruled at Taj Hotel as their first Indian 'Chef De Cuisine'.

RECIPE

 15 mins   Serves 3   hot *pav*

INGREDIENTS

1¼ kg chicken

6 medium potatoes, boiled and halved

4 large tomatoes, halved

2 medium-sized onions, finely chopped

6 green chillies or peppers

1¼ inch ginger

10 garlic cloves

1 tbsp coriander seeds

1 tsp cumin seeds

½ tsp garam masala

1 tbsp lemon juice

3 tbsp oil

Salt to taste

METHOD

Grind the ginger, garlic, garam masala, coriander seeds, cumin seeds, green chillies, lemon juice, one chopped onion and salt to a paste. Coat the chicken with the paste and allow it to marinate for two hours.

In a pan, heat oil and sauté the other chopped onion till pink. Now, add the marinated chicken and fry until both sides are brown. The chicken will need to be cooked for approximately 20 minutes.

In a separate pan, heat oil and fry the potatoes till they turn golden-brown. Drain and set aside. In the same pan, lightly fry the halved tomatoes. Do not overcook the tomatoes.

Serve the chicken on a plate with fried potatoes and tomatoes.

FISH

With a coast that flanks nearly half of our country, eating fish is a way of life. The joy of doing so is only enhanced by actually going to a fish market – a boisterous and jubilant place – and buying the fish, generally sold by the wife or relatives of the man who has himself ventured deep into the ocean to net his catch. Fish is cooked and flavoured differently as you go from the western coast to the south, or from the southern coast up to the east, which means that you can travel up and down the coast without eating the same curry twice! It's no surprise then that the rest of India has taken to eating fish with fervour and gusto

POMFRET MOILEE

You have probably heard the name of this dish before in reference to the cuisine of Kerala. Indeed, Fish Moilee is Kerala's most famous fish stew. However, the Mumbai East Indian community does the Pomfret Moilee in their own native way, often with duck, chicken or beef. Like most East Indian recipes, the Pomfret Moilee is simple and relies on the secret ingredient, bottle masala. While the Moilee can be made with other fish like mori or shark, I prefer it with pomfret. This silvery-white rhomboid is, after all, any Mumbai pescetarian's pride. And this simple, yet flavourful dish is evidence of why the pomfret holds pride of place in our cuisine.

RECIPE

30 mins   Serves 4   bread or steamed rice

INGREDIENTS

1 medium-sized pomfret

3 onions, thinly sliced into rings

3 green chillies, slivered

1 tbsp bottle masala (see page 143)

½-inch ginger, cut lengthwise

8 garlic cloves, cut lengthwise

2 tbsp ghee

½ cup water

Vinegar to taste

Salt to taste

Oil for frying

METHOD

Slice the pomfret into pieces. Wash the pomfret pieces and marinate with two tsp salt. Pour oil in a pan. Once the oil is heated, fry the pomfret pieces until they are crisp on both sides.

In a pan, heat ghee or clarified butter. Add onions, chillies, ginger and garlic. Fry them till they are golden-brown, and then add the bottle masala. Pour in half a cup of water, vinegar and salt to taste. Let it simmer for a few minutes, so that the masala cooks properly and the oil separates. Once it is cooked, add the fried fish to it. Mix it well so that all the spices and flavours blend in with the fish. Cook for a few minutes.

Serve warm.

PRAWNS ATWAN

Prawns Atwan is an East Indian Catholic dish. East Indian Catholics are the original inhabitants of what was the island of Bombay, Thana and Bassein. Then why should a community living on India's west coast be called East Indian? I have no clue, but what I do know is that this Marathi-speaking community has a distinctive cuisine – one that, like their history and culture, was once rich, but is now at the risk of being lost forever. Most of their food is slow-cooked, non-vegetarian and uses little coconut. Also, it is flavoured with that one East Indian spice called the bottle masala. It adds magic to many a dish, like this one.

RECIPE

20 mins   Serves 4   steamed rice or *fugias*

INGREDIENTS

250 gm prawns, shelled

1 tbsp bottle masala (see Page 142)

2 onions, chopped

3 green chillies, chopped

1-inch ginger, chopped

6 garlic cloves, chopped

½ cup tamarind juice

2 tbsp oil

Salt to taste

¼ cup water

Fresh coriander leaves, chopped

METHOD

Heat oil in a pan. Add ginger, garlic and green chillies and fry them for a few minutes. Add chopped onions and then fry them until they are cooked. Now add the bottle masala and tamarind pulp. Mix and cook all the ingredients.

Once the masala is cooked, add the shelled prawns. Stir the prawns and pour in ¼ cup of water. Add salt to taste. Let it simmer till the prawns are cooked and the gravy has thickened. Once the gravy is thick enough, the prawns are ready to serve. Garnish with freshly chopped coriander.

Serve hot.

CHINCHONI

Sometimes, the description of the dish is in the name itself. Chinchoni comes from *chinch*, which means tamarind in Marathi. Do I need to tell you then that this is a nice, sour, tangy fish preparation? The influences date back to when the Portuguese would pickle their fish and meat for their never-ending sea voyages. Souring agents like vinegar, kokum and tamarind were often used as preservatives. These ingredients also create an idiosyncratic and luscious piquancy when mixed with masalas. Close your eyes and imagine your palate filled with fiery red masalas in oil. Now picture balancing it with some milky coconut and a bit of sourness. You can either remain with your eyes closed or actually try making the Chinchoni.

RECIPE

 30 mins   Serves 4   steamed rice or veg *pulao*

INGREDIENTS

1 pomfret or shark, cut into pieces

250 gm coconut

6 red chillies

1 tsp cumin seeds (*jeera*)

1-inch turmeric

8 garlic cloves

Tamarind pulp

Oil for frying

Salt to taste

Water

METHOD

In a mixer, add red chillies, cumin seeds, coconut, turmeric and garlic, and grind coarsely.

In a pan, heat one tbsp of oil. Add the ground masala and fry till it is cooked. In the same pan, pour some water and tamarind pulp. Stir well.

Add the fish pieces and cook them for a few minutes. Add salt to taste. Let it simmer and cook the fish for 15 minutes. Stir continuously and cook some more until the gravy thickens.

Serve warm.

FISH KUJIT

East Indian cuisine is a unique blend of Koli, Maharashtrian and Portuguese cuisine. The Kolis were the original inhabitants of the city, the Maharashtrians were the cultural ambassadors of Mumbai and the Portuguese were the rulers of the islands. For the East Indian Marathi-speaking Christians, the mix was heady. Adapting the best of the best, they created a cuisine that was aromatic and unique.

Fish Kujit is a curry like the many hundred curries that inhabit the coastal areas of the Konkan. It is light, ambrosial and uses what I like to predominantly call green and yellow masalas. The pungency comes from peppercorn and green chillies. No red, fiery, hot chillies here.

RECIPE

 30 mins   Serves 4   steamed rice

INGREDIENTS

1 pomfret or surmai

1 large onion, thinly sliced

6 green chillies, thinly sliced

1-inch ginger, thinly sliced

2 tomatoes, thinly sliced

½ cup coconut milk

6 garlic cloves

1 tsp cumin seeds (*jeera*)

1½ tsp coriander powder

½ tsp turmeric powder

6 peppercorns

2 tbsp vinegar

2 tbsp oil

Salt to taste

METHOD

In a mixer, add garlic cloves, cumin seeds, coriander powder, turmeric powder and peppercorns. Grind these spices. In a wok, heat oil and fry the ginger, chillies and onions until they turn golden-brown.

Add the tomatoes and cook till they leave water. Now, add the ground masala. Fry for a few minutes and then add water. Cook the masala for a while until the aromas are well-blended. Now pour in the coconut milk and mix well. Add salt to taste. Finally, add the fish. Cook for a few minutes and bring it to a boil. When the curry comes to a boil, add two tbsp of vinegar and stir well.

Serve warm.

PRAWN PATHWAD

I come from a very small Maharashtrian community and we call ourselves Pathare Prabhus. We are one of the oldest communities in Mumbai and have been here for over 700 years. The cuisine of this community is quite distinctive, yet similar to that of Maharashtra. However, our vegetarian food is often embellished with the unnecessary, yet welcoming addition of shrimp and mince. Shrimp and mince add to the decadence and brazenness of our culture and food. What we call Pathwad is, in fact, what the rest of the state calls Aluwadi, or the Konkanis call Patrode or what the Gujaratis call Patrel. Rolls of taro leaves of the Colocasia plant are smeared with grain flour and stuffed with spices, tamarind and jaggery. The Pathare Prabhus add shrimp or mince or both!

RECIPE

40 mins   Serves 4–8   green and sweet tamarind chutney

INGREDIENTS

3 taro leaves

½ cup prawns, cleaned, de-veined and finely chopped

½ cup gram flour (*besan*)

½ tbsp sesame seeds

½ tbsp red chilli powder

½ tbsp garam masala

½ tsp tamarind paste

2 green chillies

¼ inch ginger

2 garlic cloves

1 tsp coriander seeds

¼ tsp jaggery

A pinch of baking soda

1–2 tbsp oil

Salt to taste

Coriander leaves, chopped

You will also need: A steamer

METHOD

Wash and clean the taro leaves. Grind chillies, ginger, garlic and coriander seeds into paste. Place the leaves upside down and flatten their veins by pressing with a rolling pin.

In a bowl, mix gram flour, ground paste, red chilli powder, garam masala, salt, soda, sesame seeds, tamarind paste, jaggery, finely chopped prawns and 1–2 tsp of water into a thick batter.

Place the largest leaf on a flat surface and apply 1–2 tsp of batter evenly over it. Layer another leaf on top of the first leaf and apply the batter. Repeat with third taro leaf. Roll the leaves from the base towards the tip.

Steam this roll in a steamer for 10–15 minutes or until you are able to insert a toothpick that is still clean on removal. Keep the rolls aside to cool. Then cut them into small pieces.

Garnish with chopped coriander leaves.

A bun-dle of joy: Hot, hot, freshly baked brun pav at Yazdani Bakery, Mumbai

PRAWN & DRUMSTICK CURRY

Vegetables together with fish make for a very healthy diet. Vegetables with a meek and mild character work perfectly with Continental and Mediterranean fish preparations. However, pairing the right fish with the right vegetable is something you can leave to the East Indian community. I have to admit that prawns with drumsticks is a killer combination as both have distinct tastes and textures. Drumsticks are mildly bitter and fleshy, while prawns add a sweetness and plumpness. Together with bottle masala, it makes for a robustness that is calmed only with coconut milk, and reignited with the sourness of tamarind.

RECIPE

 40 mins Serves 4 steamed rice or *fugias*

INGREDIENTS

1 cup prawns, shelled, cleaned and de-veined

8 drumsticks, each cut into three-inch pieces (pumpkin, cauliflower and white raddish are good alternatives)

2 onions, sliced

½ cup coconut milk

2 tsp bottle masala (see p142)

2 tbsp oil

Salt to taste

Tamarind to taste

½ cup water

METHOD

In a vessel, heat oil and add onions. Fry the onions till they are transparent. Now, add the prawns and fry them till they turn pink in colour.

Once the prawns are pink, add bottle masala and fry for a minute or so. Now, add the drumsticks. Pour the water for the gravy and add salt to taste. Cook till the drumsticks are tender.

Pour the coconut milk, stir well and cook for a few minutes. Add tamarind pulp. Stir vigorously, so that all the ingredients mix well.

Cook till the curry comes to a boil. When the curry is boiled, take the vessel off the fire.

Serve hot.

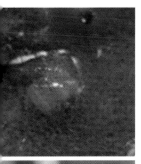

MUTTON

Not very long ago a young bride, about to be married, was in for a rude shock. In the middle of the proceedings, the groom's family suddenly halted the wedding. Instead of the usual demands like more dowry, a bigger car or more gold, they took exception to the chicken biryani that was on the menu and demanded a swap for mutton biryani. Emotions ran high and the spunky bride turned down the groom. This is a true story; the incident took place in Bangalore. I understand the groom's angst – mutton cannot be ousted by any other meat.

SHIKARI PULAO

I have never hunted for game in my life and never will. Shikar (hunting) was introduced to India by the Mughals and continued to be a royal sport for the maharajas. Even today, we encounter rare cases of this bloody sport albeit under cloak and shotgun.

I confess I am a sucker for recipes that emerged from this custom of cooking game in the jungle. Shikari Pulao was designed for exactly that. By that logic, it should've been a wham, bam, cook the ram recipe, but it's much more. After all, it's not like the maharajas and English sahibs camped and hunted in the jungles all by themselves, leaving the khansamahs and hamals behind.

RECIPE

 60 mins   Serves 4–5   green chillies or raita

INGREDIENTS

2 cups basmati rice, washed and drained

1 kg mutton

2 large onions, thinly sliced

2 large tomatoes, chopped

2 bay leaves

3 black cardamom pods

2-inch stick of cinnamon

8 cloves

1 tsp of peppercorns

½ tsp cumin powder

½ tsp coriander powder

½ tsp garam masala

1 tsp turmeric powder

1 tsp red chilli powder

1 tsp ginger paste

1 tsp garlic paste

4 tbsp ghee

Salt to taste

7 cups water

Fresh coriander leaves

METHOD

In a large vessel, boil the meat and bay leaves in four cups of water. Keep the meat covered until it is cooked and the water has completely dried. Set aside.

Heat the ghee in a frying pan. Temper all the whole spices. Add onions and fry till they turn brown.

Add ginger paste, garlic paste, tomatoes and mix well. Add all the powdered spices and fry. Pour a little water, so that the spices cook well without sticking to the pan. Add fresh coriander and continue to fry until the ghee starts to separate from the masala.

Add rice and fry for a minute or two. Add the cooked meat and three cups of water. When the water comes to a boil, lower the heat and allow the rice to simmer in the gravy until it is completely cooked and the water fully evaporated.

Serve hot.

KHEEMA PARATHA

After all, a Kheema Paratha is just minced meat stuffed in bread. As if it is the father of the Malaysian Murtabak, the brother of the Baida Kheema Roti and the stepbrother of the Italian Lasagna, they will all tell you that a Kheema Paratha is only as good as the *kheema* stuffed in it. According to me, the cipher to a great *kheema* is the choice of spices and then most importantly, resisting the temptation to pour water while cooking. You can flavour your *kheema* with all the masalas in the world, but I personally favour the green masalas.

RECIPE

 60 mins   Serves 4   butter, mango pickle or yoghurt

INGREDIENTS

The Stuffing

½ kg mutton, minced

1 onion, finely chopped

1½ tbsp ginger-garlic paste

4 green chillies, finely chopped or paste

½ tsp cumin seeds (*jeera*)

½ tsp bishop's weed (*ajwain*)

1 tsp cumin powder

1 tbsp coriander powder

A pinch of garam masala

Salt to taste

1 tbsp oil

1 tbsp lemon juice

Coriander, finely chopped

The Paratha

2 cups wheat flour

3 tbsp plain yoghurt

Oil or ghee

METHOD

Heat oil in a pan on medium flame. Add cumin seeds and fry for a minute. Add chopped onions and fry till they turn golden-brown.

Add ginger-garlic paste and fry for a minute. Add the minced mutton along with all the powdered spices. Cook for a few minutes till the oil separates from it and the meat is tender. Do not pour water. Remove from flame and keep aside to cool.

Add wheat flour and curd in a bowl. Knead the dough just like you would for a chapati. Shape it into ten small balls. On a floured surface, roll out each ball to medium-sized parathas.

Place cooked meat stuffing in the centre of the paratha. Lift paratha's edges to the centre to cover the stuffing. Flatten it out again first with your hand and then a rolling pin. Heat a tava or griddle. Gently place the paratha. When it turns brown, smear oil or ghee around the edges. Roast until both sides are golden-brown.

GREEN KHEEMA

I'm fastidious, fussy and finicky when it comes to . I like it green. It's the way the remaining few Chiliya restaurants in Mumbai make it, with green chillies and coriander. The Muslim Chiliya Momins are originally from the villages of north Gujarat. In the early 50s and 60s, they set up cafés and eateries similar in style to that of the Irani joints, but with Muslim food. You could probably find a few of them still left in Mumbai and some in Ahmedabad. Look for names like New Lucky Restaurant, Olympia, Alla-Behli, Paramount, Bagdadi or simply, Patel Restaurant. You'll find Green Kheema for sure. I like a full portion of it with sunny-side up eggs. Bear in mind, however, that it's a breakfast dish, so most restaurants won't serve it to you after 9 AM.

RECIPE

40 mins | Serves 4-6 | hot bread or chapatis

INGREDIENTS

1 kg ground mutton mince

3 medium onions, thinly sliced

2 medium onions, cut in chunks

5 green chillies, split and de-seeded

4 garlic cloves, finely chopped

1 bay leaf

1 stick cinnamon

4–5 cloves

½ tsp turmeric powder

½ tsp black peppercorns

½ tsp cumin seeds

1 cup plain yoghurt

3 tbsp ghee

A bunch of fresh coriander leaves, chopped

You will also need: a heavy pot

METHOD

In a bowl, combine the minced mutton, yoghurt, salt, turmeric powder and cumin seeds. Mix it well and set aside for an hour.

In a heavy pot, heat the ghee and add the bay leaf, peppercorns and cloves. Let them splutter, then add thinly sliced onions. Cook the onions till they turn golden-brown.

Add the minced mixture and sauté well. Cook the mutton on medium flame till it releases water. Then add the slit and de-seeded green chillies, onion chunks and finely chopped garlic and mix well. Continue cooking till all of the liquid has evaporated and the meat is tender. Garnish with freshly squeezed lime juice and chopped coriander.

Serve hot.

ABEDA'S NIHARI

Cooking mutton can sometimes seem like a pain. After an hour of cooking, you often find the meat still rubbery and uncooked. Then, you try shoving the whole thing into a pressure cooker and sometimes, even that doesn't work. The key is selecting the right mutton – light pink, firm, fine-grained, velvety and most importantly, moist. Then, choose a cut of mutton depending on how you plan to cook it. For quick-cooking, choose chops or cutlets. For slow-cooking, the shoulder and shank are good. Nihari is slow-cooked mutton shanks in rich masalas. On the streets of Lucknow and Agra, it is a staple breakfast. It's slow-cooked all night and served just as the sun rises.

RECIPE

 2 mins   Serves 4–6   hot bread or naan

INGREDIENTS

1 kg mutton (with bones)
3 medium onions, thinly sliced
2 tbsp flour
1 small piece dry ginger
2 small white cardamomas
2 bay leaves & 1 cinnamon stick
2 tsp garam masala
2 tbsp fennel seeds, powdered
1 tsp red chilli powder
2 pinches of nutmeg (jaiphal)
½ tsp turmeric powder
1 small piece black salt
1 tbsp garlic paste & 1 tbsp ginger paste
½ cup plain yoghurt
½ cup ghee or cooking oil
Salt to taste

Garnish

1 medium onion, sliced and fried
3 green chillies, sliced
2-inch piece of ginger, thinly sliced
Coriander leaves, chopped

METHOD

In a pot, heat the ghee or cooking oil. When it is hot, add in the sliced onions. On medium heat, fry the onions till golden-brown. Remove and cool the onions on a paper tissue. Crush the onions and keep aside.

In the same oil/ghee, fry the mutton, garam masala, yoghurt, ginger paste, garlic paste, crushed fried onions, salt, red chilli powder, bay leaves, cinnamon and turmeric powder. Stir continuously till the oil separates. Then add in the nutmeg, cardamoms, aniseeds and black salt and cook them. Pour enough water to cover the meat. Cook the meat on a low flame for two hrs or till it is tender. Once the meat is tender, add flour and cook on low heat for about another ten minutes.

Garnish with fried onions, freshly chopped coriander leaves, green chillies and ginger strips.

EGG FRIED MUTTON CHOPS

The Parsis do it and the Dawoodi Bohras do it. And they did it well before Kentucky fried chicken crowed one early morning in the 30s. Frying meat coated with egg batter is a tradition that is revered and relished.

At my friend Pesi's home, his mom would pick out pieces from the previous night's Jardaloo ma Ghosht (apricot meat stew), crumb them, dip them in egg batter and deep-fry them for the next meal. So you have the succulent marination of last night's masalas, but freshly and crisply fried for another meal. To me, that idea is just genius. The same applies to Egg Fried Mutton Chops. Instead of leftover pieces of meat, you choose luscious ribs, cook them and egg fry them.

RECIPE

60 mins   Serves 6   onions and lemon

INGREDIENTS

The Mutton
1 kg mutton ribs
2 eggs
1 cup flour
2 tbsp plain yoghurt
250 ml whole milk
1 tbsp lemon juice
Salt to taste
Oil for frying
½ litre water

The Potli
¼ tsp baking powder
1-inch ginger, sliced
2-inch cinnamon stick
1 tbsp aniseeds, powdered

Garnish
Sliced onions
Slices of lemon
Mint leaves

METHOD

Wash mutton ribs and dry them well. Marinate the ribs in salt and lemon juice for half an hour. Take ginger, cinnamon and aniseeds in a clean white cloth. Tie the cloth and make a *potli* (small bundle). In a pot, heat milk and half a litre of water. Then add the meat and soak in the *potli*. Cook until the mutton is tender.

Drain once tender. Squeeze the spice bundle to extract maximum flavour and discard. Reserve the stock.

In a bowl, sieve the flour, baking powder and salt together. Add the yoghurt and pour stock enough to make a batter of thick consistency. In another bowl, beat the eggs and keep aside.

For frying, heat oil in a pan. Dip the mutton pieces first in the batter, then in the beaten eggs. Deep-fry until golden-brown.

Serve hot.

After a big meal outside the legendary palace of meat, Karim's, Jama Masjid, Old Delhi.

MUTTON DO PIAZA

The city of Mumbai was quieter in the 60s and 70s. On dining-out weekends, our parents took us to places like Gaylord near Brabourne Stadium, Horse Shoe at Colaba Causeway, Berry's at Churchgate, Gulmarg and Kwality's at Kemps Corner and Talk-of-the-Town on Marine Drive. They all served, among other things, Indian cuisine, but the dishes they served have slowly vanished. Mutton Do Piaza is one of them. It is mutton cooked with two kinds of onions. The dish arrives at your table with chunky pieces of meat cooked in thick onion gravy with chunkier pieces of soft, translucent whole onion.

RECIPE

60 mins   Serves 4   naan or hot bread

INGREDIENTS

500 gm mutton

500 gm onions, chopped

2 tbsp ghee or oil

1 cup plain yoghurt, beaten

1 tsp garlic, chopped

2 bay leaves

4 green cardamoms

2-inch cinnamon stick

½ tsp cumin seeds (*jeera*)

1 tsp dry ginger powder

1 tsp coriander powder

1 tsp red chilli powder

1 tsp garam masala

Salt to taste

Coriander leaves for garnish

METHOD

In a pan, heat ghee or oil. Add the cumin seeds, bay leaves, cinnamon stick and green cardamoms and fry for a minute.

Then, add the chopped onions and garlic. Cook the onions till they turn golden-brown. In a bowl, lightly beat the yogurt. Once the onions are golden-brown, add the lightly beaten yogHurt, salt, red chilli powder, garam masala, coriander powder and dry ginger powder.

Fry the masalas till they are fragrant and

well-cooked, then add the mutton pieces. Mix the mutton and the masalas well. Cook till the mutton is tender. Garnish with freshly chopped coriander leaves.

Mutton Do Piaza is ready to serve.

MUTTON KHUDDI

The East Indian community of Mumbai is one of the city's oldest settlers. In the by-lanes of Girgaum, in the villages of Bandra, in the now urbanized areas of Amboli, Andheri, Vakola and Marol, you can still find the community holding onto their old tiled-roof homes and backyards. Evangelized by the Portuguese and converted to Christianity in the Pre-British era, the East Indians are Marathi-speaking folk, who still preserve their pre-Christian Marathi culture and traditions, including their food. While a few of their dishes are similar to their fellow Christian Goans, most of their food is distinctive. The Mutton Khuddi, for example, is a simple enough dish made with basic spices, coconut, green chillies and the bottle masala (recipe on p22).

RECIPE

 60 mins   Serves 6   steamed rice or

INGREDIENTS

1 kg mutton

2 potatoes

4 medium onions, chopped

4 green chillies

¼ coconut, in pieces or scraped

½ cup tamarind juice

2 tbsp ghee

1 tbsp bottle masala (see page 142)

Garam masala to taste

Salt to taste

Water

METHOD

In a pan, roast chopped onions, green chillies and scraped coconut. Cool and grind them.

In a pan, heat two tbsp of ghee and fry the ground masala until fragrant. Then add one tbsp of bottle masala. Let it cook properly till the oil separates from the masala.

Add cubed meat pieces. Fry the meat and mix well. Pour in enough water for the meat to cook. Add salt to taste and cook till the meat is tender. Add chopped potatoes.

When cooked, add freshly squeezed sour lime or tamarind juice. For added flavour, add garam masala.

Serve warm.

MINCE POTATO CHOPS with MINT

For want of a better definition, let's call this a croquette or a stuffed Aloo Tikki. It's a small patty or ball of mashed potatoes, stuffed with minced meat, usually breaded, egg-washed and deep-fried. The chop is quite common among most Indian communities. You can stuff the potato with green peas, corn, mixed vegetables, paneer, chopped boiled egg, cheese, ham, chicken-in-white-sauce or even leftover food. Bengal makes a great macher chop (fish chop), the Goans do it with spicy vinegary mince, and my mom makes it with creamy mashed potatoes stuffed with mushy peas and green chutney.

RECIPE

 60 mins
 Serves 4
tomato ketchup

INGREDIENTS

The Chops

250 gm lamb, minced & 500 gm potatoes

2 medium onions, finely chopped

2 tomatoes or 2 cups tomato puree

1 cup mint leaves, finely chopped

2 tbsp garlic cloves, finely minced

1 tbsp grated ginger

1 tbsp coriander powder

1 tsp cumin powder, ½ tsp red chilli powder & 1 tsp turmeric powder

½ tsp pepper powder

1 tsp garam masala

A pinch of nutmeg and green cardamom powder

1 tbsp sugarcane vinegar

4 tbsp vegetable oil & Salt to taste

A few coriander leaves, finely chopped

Dipping, Rolling & Frying

1 egg, lightly beaten

1 cup bread crumbs

2½ tbsp cornflour & Oil

METHOD

Heat four tbsp of oil in a pan. On medium flame, sauté onions till soft and translucent. Add ginger and garlic. Sauté till the rawness disappears. Add all the dry spice powders, sugar and tomatoes. Sauté till tomatoes are soft. Add lamb mince and stir well. Cover and slow-cook for 25 minutes. Add chopped mint leaves, nutmeg and cardamom powder. Stir occasionally and sprinkle water or oil, if mince is turning dry. Pour some vinegar and add salt to taste. Cook lamb until dry. Sprinkle chopped coriander and mix well. Keep aside to cool.

Wash potatoes and boil them in their jackets in a pressure cooker till tender. Drain, peel and mash the potatoes. Form a ball out of a handful and make a hollow in it to fill with the mince stuffing. Then form a smooth, well-shaped round cutlet. Evenly dip and coat each potato chop in the beaten egg and roll in the prepared bread crumbs. Refrigerate for about 20 minutes. Then deep-fry till lightly golden.

EDDIE'S MUTTON STEW

The history of stews can be traced back to a time when there were no cooking vessels. Every culture has its own version of stew, the most famous of which is the Irish Stew. There's also Cassoulet or Ratatouille from France, Caldeirada from Portugal, Gheimeh from Iran, or closer home, the rich, fragrant Kerala Ishtew.

My recipe below is the Anglo-Indian version. Anglo-Indian cooking is now a near-forgotten tradition that emerged and evolved during the British Raj in India. The hangover from the Raj stayed on for many years after Independence, and so did Eddie, the butler-cum-cook at my great-uncle's home. This is his recipe from my memory, spiced with fragrant garam masala.

RECIPE

60 mins   Serves 6   hot bread or steamed rice

INGREDIENTS

½ kg mutton

2 potatoes, cut lengthwise

2 onions, finely chopped

1 piece ginger, finely chopped

4 garlic cloves, finely chopped

2 green chillies, finely chopped

2 cups chicken or vegetable stock

1 tsp flour

10–12 whole peppercorns

2 cloves

2 cardamoms

1 tsp ground pepper

2 cinnamon sticks

2 tbsp ghee

Salt to taste

METHOD

In a pan, fry cut pieces of meat in a warm tbsp of ghee, till meat is seared and changes colour. Remove from pan.

In the same pan, warm a tbsp of ghee. Fry the ginger and garlic and add cloves, cinnamon and cardamoms. Next, add the meat and stir-fry for a minute. Stir in a tbsp of flour. Add the freshly ground pepper, too, and pour in the stock. Add the cut potatoes and salt to taste. Slow-cook till done.

Serve warm.

[As an option, you can add sliced carrots, French beans and halved tomatoes to the stew.]

BEEF

To say that Indians do not eat beef may be a gross generalization. Nearly 72 communities in Kerala prefer beef to expensive mutton or chicken. Beef also features quite prominently in Goan cuisine.

There is nothing that can match the taste of Nadan Erachi Ularthiyathu (Kerala Beef Fry), or Bade ka Seekh Kebab from Mohammad Ali Road, or for that matter Goan Potato Chops.

PAKISTANI POT ROAST FILLETS

Until a few years ago, India and Pakistan were one country. Then, can Pakistani food be so different from its neighbouring cuisine? The food is similar, but over the years, differences have developed. Pakistanis eat more meat than us, and vegetables and lentils are often reserved for sides. In terms of taste, the recipes may vary from region to region and from kitchen to kitchen. The essentials of north Indian and Pakistani cooking remain pretty much the same, except that in many regions of India, we don't eat beef. That's where they score over us.

RECIPE

 60 mins   Serves 4   steamed rice or hot naan

INGREDIENTS

1 kg round steak, cut into pieces

1 medium onion, thinly sliced

1 cup plain yoghurt

1 tsp ginger-garlic paste

1½ tbsp lemon juice

2 tsp crushed red chilli flakes

½ tsp black cumin, ground

½ tsp cloves, ground

¼ tsp turmeric powder

¾ cup vegetable oil

Salt to taste

Coriander and sliced green chillies for garnish

METHOD

In a medium bowl, add yoghurt, ginger-garlic paste, red chilli flakes, cumin, cloves, turmeric and salt and mix well. Add the meat and mix until it is evenly coated with the mixture. Set aside for 15 minutes.

In a large heavy pan, heat enough oil for frying. Once the oil is hot enough, add thinly sliced onions and fry them until they are golden-brown.

Once the onions are golden-brown, remove one tbsp of onion and set aside for garnish. Reduce the flame. Place meat in the pan, cover it and cook until tender. Pour water while cooking, if required. Pour in freshly squeezed lemon juice and let it simmer for ten minutes.

Garnish with freshly chopped coriander, green chillies and reserved fried onion.

Serve hot.

Crunching on a scrumptious drumstick of Chicken Farcha at Parsi da Dhaba, Talasari, Mumbai-Gujarat Highway

KERALA BEEF FRY

God's own country, Kerala, is very hot, but it is blessed with fish, vanilla, cocoa, cinnamon, coconut, toddy and nutmeg. It seems as though God created this place for great food. We then went and divided the people of this place into Hindus, Muslims and Christians, but the advantage of this is that it offers you three distinctive cuisines, each more delicious than the other. Among beef-eaters in Kerala, the Kerala Beef Fry or Olathirachi, as it is known, is a staple. You can eat it with rice, appams or the way I like it, with steamed tapioca.

RECIPE

60 mins   Serves 4   steamed rice or malbari parathas

INGREDIENTS

½ kg beef

2 large onions, thinly sliced

1-inch ginger

8 garlic cloves

8–10 cloves

Few curry leaves

6 tbsp grated coconut

3 tsp red chilli powder

2½ tsp coriander powder

1 tsp cumin powder

2 tsp pepper powder

2 one-inch cinnamon sticks

3 tsp vinegar

Coconut oil

Salt to taste

Coconut, sliced into rings

METHOD

Wash, clean and cut the beef into small pieces. Pound cinnamon and cloves and keep it aside. In a bowl, add all the dry spice powders and mix with salt and vinegar. Add the spice mixture to the beef and mix well.

Finely chop the ginger and garlic and mix with the beef. Now add vinegar and keep it aside. Meanwhile, slice coconut rings and deep-fry in hot oil till they turn brown. Drain and keep aside for garnish.

Add it to the beef. Heat oil in a pan. Fry thinly sliced onions and grated coconut till they turn brown. Drain and keep aside.

Pressure-cook the marinated beef till tender. Heat oil in a pan, temper with shredded curry leaves and throw in the pressure cooked beef along with the gravy. Cook beef till the curry thickens.

Serve beef ganished with fried onions and fried coconut rings.

CHORIZRO PULAO WITH DRY FRUITS

You would need to be a really bad cook to screw up Goa sausages. You can buy them fully spiced and cured in their covers, and the true Goan says that all you have to do is chop and boil them. Some add onion and potato to the mix to make it more flavoursome, while others will ruin everything by adding capsicum and tomato. The Willingdon Club in Mumbai makes great Sausage Pulao with the very same Goa sausages. Personally, I like to add a bit of dry fruit to the Sausage Pulao to balance out the pungency and tartness. I think it works quite well.

RECIPE

 45 mins   Serves 4–6   fried potato chips

INGREDIENTS

The Pulao
10 Goan sausages
½ kg Basmati rice
2 medium onions, sliced
2 medium tomatoes, sliced
3 green chillies
8 garlic cloves, finely chopped
5 cloves
1 tsp turmeric powder
2 bay leaves
5 peppercorns
2 cinnamon sticks
2 green cardamoms
1 black cardamom, coarsely crushed
½ tsp cumin seeds (jeera)
A pinch of sugar
1 tbsp fresh coriander leaves
2 tbsp vegetable oil
Salt to taste
Water

Garnish
Fresh coriander leaves, chopped
½ cup fried cashews, onions and raisins

METHOD

Wash and soak rice for about 15–20 minutes. Cut the strings and split the casing of the sausage beads open. Transfer the meat to a bowl.

Heat oil in a pressure cooker and put in all of the spices. Let them crackle and splutter. Add finely chopped garlic, slit green chillies and turmeric powder. Sauté till it releases their aroma. Add sliced onions and sauté till light brown. Add sliced tomatoes and sauté till soft.

Toss in and fry the reserved sausage meat on low heat. Gently mix in the rice and cook till it is well fried. Pour just enough water to cover the rice. Do not pour too much water or the pulao will become too soft.

Add a pinch of sugar, coriander leaves and salt to taste. Fix the cooker lid and cook for up to two whistles. Release steam immediately. Open the lid and let the pulao rest for about ten minutes.

Garnish with fried onions, chopped coriander leaves and dry fruits. Serve hot.

DESSERT

Why on earth is dessert, or the sweet-dish as we also know it, reserved for the end of the meal? If I had my way, I'd start with dessert, end with dessert and have some even midway through my meal. Dessert as a finale is a western concept. In India, sweets are often served along with the food. Our love for dessert is perpetual. We have explored, experimented and created boundless kinds of desserts. They are also an integral part of religion, rituals and our daily lives.

SEV BADAM BURFI

If you are Sindhi, you know what Sev Badam Burfi is. It's a staple for any celebration, be it a wedding, birthday or a spurt in your finances. It's a unique *halva* (pudding) that is both sweet and savoury. It's simple to make and just divine.

The Sindhi community fled from Pakistan during the Partition, and now live in different parts of the country and the world. A lot of Sindhi food still acknowledges its Muslim influences, especially where sweets are concerned. Praghri or *khaja*-like puff pastry and *sev*, or *seviyan* (vermicelli), are quite similar in terms of how they are made in Pakistan. The original recipe for Sev Badam Burfi or Singhar Burfi calls for unsalted sev, but I like to make it with salted *sev*.

RECIPE

 30 mins   Serves 4-5   *pista*, rose petals and *gulkand*

INGREDIENTS

250 gm *sev*, fried and unsalted from the *farsan* walla

250 gm khoya (condensed milk or mawa)

50 gm almonds, slivered

250 gm sugar

250 ml water

Saffron strands, soaked in milk

½ tsp cardamom powder

You will also need: A greased thali (plate)

METHOD

In a wok, pour the water and mix in the sugar. Boil till the sugar has dissolved. Add khoya and mix till it is melted. Stir gently till all the ingredients are well blended. Keep stirring and add saffron and cardamom powder.

Now add the sev. Stir gently and add half the almonds. Mix well till it starts to thicken. Once it thickens, pour this mixture in a greased thali. Garnish with the remaining almonds. Set aside and cool for 30 minutes.

Once the mixture has cooled, cut into squares of desired size and serve.

TIPSY PUDDING

There is not a captain, lieutenant, brigadier, general, admiral, air marshal or cadet in the Indian Armed Forces who has not tasted Tipsy Pudding. Every graduate from the National Defence Academy (NDA) has been served this iconic pudding on special occasions. While the Academy has made this pudding its own, Tipsy Pudding is a variation of the traditional Trifle Pudding. A rich, cold pudding, a layered melange of sponge cake soaked in sherry, brandy or rum and smothered with jelly, custard and cream, it is the quintessential English dessert. However, jelly being a controversial ingredient, has been dropped at the NDA. But Tipsy Pudding doesn't need it and the cadets don't miss it.

RECIPE

40 mins   Serves 4–6   vanilla ice cream

INGREDIENTS

The Cake

250 gm sponge cake

4 tsp rum or sherry

1 cup lime juice

1 cup fruit juice

50 gm raisins

50 gm cashewnuts, chopped

50 gm walnuts, chopped

The Custard

5 egg yolks

2 cups milk

¼ tsp oil

4 tsp powdered sugar

½ tsp vanilla essence

Garnish

1 cup mixed crystallized fruits, chopped

1 cup mixed nuts

METHOD

Slice the sponge cake into two layers. Place the first layer on the serving dish, ensuring it fits the dish well. Mix half the rum/sherry, lime juice and fruit juice. Sprinkle the remaining onto the sponge layer, such that the cake soaks the liquids well. Mix half the raisins and walnuts and spread over the sponge. Repeat the process while adding the second layer to the sponge cake.

In a pan, beat the egg yolks and sugar and mix well. Now add the milk. Mix well. In a large pan, boil water. Now place the egg mixture over this pan and stir gently and continuously. Whisk until the custard is thickened. Do not boil or else it will curdle. Now mix in vanilla essence and keep whisking until cool.

Pour the custard over the sponge cake and decorate with crystallized fruits and nuts.

VANILLA SHEERMAL

Sheermal is best described as a flaming orange, subtly sweet, layered paratha. It's such a popular bread in Lucknow, that they've named a street after it – Sheermal-wale Galli. A thick mist of flour engulfs you as you stroll into this old part of Lucknow. The aroma of fresh baking momentarily deodorizes the mustiness of this ancient artery. And lo and behold, in the foreground of underground tandoors, you spot piles of flat cane baskets with sunset-coloured, mildly sweet parathas. Sheermals are being sold by the dozens for patrons to eat with their home-cooked *kevda* (pandamus flower essence), flavoured *quormas*, *saalans* (types of curry) and *galavatis* (a type of kebab). My poison is more vanilla. It adds that little something to make me smile.

RECIPE

 5 hrs   Serves 4   cold *rabri*

INGREDIENTS

3 cups refined wheat flour (maida)

1 cup whole fat milk

1 tsp sugar

¾ cup ghee

½ tsp vanilla essence

Salt to taste

A few strands of saffron, soaked in 2 tbsp milk

You will also need: A heavy iron pan, griddle or tava.

METHOD

In a large bowl, sift together flour and salt. Sprinkle in the sugar and pour the melted ghee. Pouring milk a little at a time, knead it into soft dough. Cover it with a moist cloth and set aside for two hours.

Knead the dough again and set aside for another two hours. Knead again and divide into seven parts. In a small bowl, rub saffron strands in milk and add vanilla essence.

Heat an inverted heavy iron pan on the stovetop. Turn on the second flame alongside. Roll out the dough into thick round parathas. Prick it all over with a fork.

Slap it onto the inverted pan and bake till brown. Shift the parantha to the open flame. Flip it a few times until it is cooked.

Shift the sheermal back onto the inverted pan. Then, using your fingers, splash with saffron milk and vanilla essence mix. Leave it for a minute or so. Remove and serve warm.

You know reality is better than TV when you find yourself licking your fork clean at Café Zoe, Parel, Mumbai

CROISSANT PUDDING

This is essentially a classic bread-and-butter pudding, but instead of using bread slices, the recipe uses butter croissants. The classic bread pudding found its origins among those who did not want to waste stale bread, but put it to good use instead. According to me, bread-and-butter pudding is comfort food and there is no pudding I like better. The key to a good pudding, however, lies in the custard. Custard can go terribly wrong; it can be thin, lumpy or smell strongly of egg. I shudder at the very thought of it.

If well-made, Croissant Pudding tastes heavenly with either crème anglaise, whipped cream or any vanilla-based sauce. Oh, I miss my grandmom!

RECIPE

 60 mins

 Serves 4–6

  crème anglaise or vanilla custard

INGREDIENTS

4 butter or plain croissants

2 eggs

3 tbsp butter

2 cups milk

3 tbsp almonds, sliced

1 cup sugar

A pinch of salt

METHOD

Preheat oven to 300 degrees Fahrenheit. In a large bowl, whisk together eggs, sugar, milk and salt until well blended. Add the croissants and coat them well in the mixture. Let the croissants sit for about ten minutes, so that they absorb some of the liquid.

Grease a baking dish with butter. Pour the egg and croissant mixture into the baking dish. Garnish with almonds. Bake for 40–50 minutes. To check if it is done, prick with a fork. If the fork comes out clean, it is done. Cool and serve.

ANDAY KA HALWA

I first came across Anday ka Halwa tucked away at the bottom of a dessert menu, overshadowed by Sheer Khurma, Seviyan and Kheer at a restaurant called Al Amir, at Ghitorni Chowk in Delhi. I then grasped that this was a traditional dessert, popular for over centuries in Muslim-ruled states, like Hyderabad. But like most traditional delicacies, one cannot really attribute its nativity to just one place. At first, just the thought of making a halwa out of eggs may sound preposterous and vile. But I guarantee that once it is done, the halwa tastes absolutely divine without the slightest hint of an eggy flavour.

RECIPE

 15 mins

 Serves 4

 paratha, puri or chapati

INGREDIENTS

6 eggs

500 gm khoya (condensed milk or *mawa*)

2 cups sugar

½ cup almonds and pistachios, finely crushed

6 green cardamoms, ground

1½ cup ghee or oil

A pinch of yellow food colouring or saffron

2 tbsp ghee or oil (for blending)

Silver foil for garnish

METHOD

Beat the eggs in a large bowl well till the white and yolk form a consistent liquid. Now, pour it into a blender. Add the milk solids, sugar, cardamom powder and a pinch of yellow food colouring. Blend this mixture till it turns smooth.

Pour the two tbsp of ghee or oil into the mixture and blend well. Now, pour 1½ cups of ghee or oil in a pan. Once the oil or ghee is heated, pour the egg and milk blend. Cook well by stirring continuously, till the oil begins to separate and a grainy texture is formed. Then add coarsely chopped almonds and pistachios. Mix them well into the mixture and cook for a minute or two. Transfer the *halwa* to a tray and garnish with silver foil.

Serve warm.

Short menu with hugely satisfying dishes at Martin's, Colaba, Mumbai

SIDES

In any western table setting, there is always a smaller quarter plate, used for salad or bread or what they call a 'side'. In India, however, be it a wedge of lemon, a plump green chilli or our prodigious array of achars and chutneys, we like our sides right there in the main plate. They revitalize the flavours of the food and wake up our sluggish tastebuds.

CHUTNEY

When dining at any Indian restaurant, chutney and achar (pickle) normally arrive at your table before the starters and main course, possibly with some sliced onion and roasted papad. The pickle is either made of lime or mixed vegetables and the chutney is invariably green with mint and coriander. If the restaurant is posh, then the green chutney will be beaten through with yoghurt and spices. Impatient for the meal, I proceeded with my attack. While the chutney and pickle is are accompaniments, I often make a whole meal out of them, mixing the papad with chutney, dipping the papad in the pickle, sprinkling pepper on the onion rings and squeezing lime on everything. By the time the meal has arrived, I have this satiated look on my face.

We just love our chutneys, and we have dozens of varieties. Our chutneys and pickles can be raw or cooked, thin or chunky, firm or mushy and can be made of pretty much anything – fruit or vegetables or both.

On a road trip from Delhi to Chandigarh one fine morning, I got my lesson on pickles. On nearing Panipat, I stopped at a dhaba (roadside eatery) for breakfast and there was a pickle shop. I had never seen so many pickle jars before. There were over a 100 homemade varieties – mango, lemon, ginger, chilli, carrot, mushroom, nandru, red-chilli-green-chilli stuffed, pancharanga (5 ingredients), awla (Indian gooseberry), bamboo shoot, sweet or sour, spicy or mild – you name it, they pickled it.

On the other end of the spectrum is a homestay in Madikeri, Coorg. The Coorgi ladies are proud of their variety of pickles. Mutton, chicken, pork, bamboo shoot, lime, date, bitter lime, garlic, red pepper in salt, fish, picquin chilli in salt or dry mango pickle, they have it all.

Every state in India has its own variety of pickles. Some preserved in groundnut oil, some in mustard oil, others in vinegar or just brine. But the king in my books is the Parsi Lagan nu Achar. It's called an achar, but it is a pickle-cum-jam-cum-chutney, rich with meva (dry fruits). It's as though this pickle has preserved the Persian origins with its carrots, raisins, apricots, dates, ginger, dried bora berries, jaggery, malt vinegar, sugarcane vinegar, black pepper, cinnamon, cloves, nutmeg, cardamom and more.

GINGER GARLIC CHUTNEY

 25 mins   Serves 4–6   just about anything

RECIPE

INGREDIENTS

1 cup freshly grated coconut

2 tbsp fried Bengal gram (chana dal)

4 onions, chopped

2 garlic cloves

1 piece fresh ginger

2 green chillies

2 red chillies

1 small ball of tamarind

½ tsp mustard seeds

A pinch asafoetida powder

1 tsp oil

1 tsp salt

A few curry leaves

METHOD

Put all the ingredients, except mustard seeds, asafoetida and curry leaves, in a mixer. Add water and grind to a thick paste. In a small pan, add oil. Add mustard seeds, asafoetida and curry leaves. Let them splutter. Temper the paste with it. Shift the chutney to a glass bowl or jar.

Eat fresh.

PEAR CHUTNEY

 30 mins   Serves 4–8   chapati and a south Indian meal

RECIPE

INGREDIENTS

1 ripe pear

2–3 one-inch fresh ginger pieces

4–5 red chillies

1 tbsp Bengal gram (chana dal)

1 tbsp split white gram dal (urad dal)

Paste of a small ball of tamarind

A pinch of asafoetida

2 tsp oil

Salt to taste

METHOD

Peel the skin from the pear and cut it into small pieces. Peel the ginger and cut it into small pieces as well. In a kadai or wok, heat the oil. When it is hot, add Bengal gram, asafoetida and urad dal. Fry till they turn golden-brown. Then, add tamarind paste and fry for a few seconds.

Now, add the ginger pieces and fry for a few seconds. Mix in the red chillies and fry for another few seconds. Finally, add and fry pear pieces for a few more seconds. Take it off the flame and keep aside to cool. Sprinkle some salt and mix well. In a mixer, grind it to a coarse paste.

Store in a glass container.

LAGAN NU ACHAAR

 60 mins   Serves 4–8   a parsi meal, biryani or hot roti

RECIPE

INGREDIENTS

1 kg carrots, grated

150 gm seedless raisins

150 gm dried apricots

150 gm dried dates, chopped

25 gm dried ginger, sliced

25 gm dried round red chillies

50 gm dried garlic, sliced

1 kg sugar

¼ kg jaggery

½ bottle sugarcane vinegar

1 tbsp chilli powder

1 tbsp black pepper powder

2 tbsp garam masala

Salt to taste

METHOD

Combine carrots, sugar, jaggery and vinegar in a large saucepan. Mix and cook on a low flame until the carrots turn soft. Stir in ginger, garlic and salt. Cook until the mixture gets sticky. Now mix dates, red chillies, raisins and apricots. Bring to a boil on low flame.

Mix in chilli powder, black pepper and garam masala. Cool and store in a glass container and refrigerate. It lasts for a week or so.

Exploring each bite, savouring the flavour, while pleasing all senses on the streets of Mumbai, Mohammad Ali Road.

PATHARE PRABHU CHUTNEY

 25 mins   Serves 4–8   *puran poli* and a maharashtrian meal

RECIPE

INGREDIENTS

1 tbsp Pathare Prabhu sambar masala

½ tsp turmeric powder

1 tsp red chilli powder

3 tbsp roasted peanut powder

1 tsp mustard seeds

¼ tsp cumin seeds (jeera)

2 tbsp jaggery

3 tbsp raisins

2 tbsp cashewnuts

3 tbsp peanuts

2 tbsp fresh coconut slices

2 green chillies, chopped

A pinch of asafoetida

A few curry leaves

METHOD

Heat oil in a pan, add mustard seeds and asafoetida. When mustard seeds start popping, add cumin seeds, curry leaves, green chillies and fresh coconut slices. Cook until slightly coloured. Add turmeric powder, red chilli powder, Pathare Prabhu sambar masala and fry well. Add peanuts, cashewnuts and raisins. Sauté till they get a nice colour. Add 1½ cups of water and salt. Add jaggery when cashewnuts are soft. Cook for 10–12 minutes or until nuts become tender. Mix roasted peanut powder. Then, cook for about 3–4 minutes on low heat.

PANCHAMRUT DRINK

I just made this up. Well, not really. I'm no master chef to be dreaming up recipes, but I can transform the existing ones. In most Maharashtrian homes, when you perform a Satyanarayan Puja, an offering of five foods is made to the gods. The idol of the God is bathed with these five foods. Panch is "five" in Sanskrit and amrut is "nectar". At the end of the puja, a spoonful of this mixture is offered as prashad. As a kid, I loved it so much, that a spoonful just wasn't enough. So, I tried making a glassful and created a refreshing, tasty beverage, best had chilled.

 15 mins   Serves 4   serve chilled

RECIPE

INGREDIENTS

2½ cup freshly whisked plain yoghurt

1 cup cold milk

2 tsp sugar

1 tbsp honey

3–4 tulsi leaves

METHOD

In a large bowl, take whisked plain yoghurt and add milk, sugar and honey. Whisk all the ingredients well with a spoon. Now add the tulsi leaves. Mix in a blender till you get a smooth paste. Serve cold.

MASALAS

Masala is nothing short of magic. When I was a child, once a year in our South Mumbai home, women in nine-yard saris would come to roast and fry spices in huge *kadhais*, making our eyes smart, noses leak and clothes smell like a baniya shop. The women, jewellery dangling from neck, nose and wrist, like the three witches from Macbeth, would chant and pound around a cauldron. They were like alchemists pulling off some devious concoctions. It's the alchemy of masalas that adds a touch of wizardry to anything you cook.

BOTTLE MASALA

My most vivid childhood memory is of my grandmother commissioning the annual masala preparation. My grandmother would carefully measure out the spices and sari-clad women would roast and then pound them in large mortars, the rhythm of which still plays in my mind. Bottle masala is made in the same manner today, now including the East Indian spice mix. Its 20–25 ingredients would be set out to dry during the relatively warm month of March to give the masala its distinctive flavour. Once ready, the masalas are stored in empty beer bottles. Hence, the name bottle masala. The secret to lasting flavour is to use beer bottles made of amber-tinted glass, that prevents light from destroying the aroma and freshness of the masalas.

RECIPE

 60 mins · Serves 6–8 · just about anything

INGREDIENTS

3 kg dry Kashmiri red chillies
750 gm coriander powder
250 gm turmeric powder
250 gm sesame seeds
125 gm cumin seeds (*jeera*)
10 gm caraway seeds (*shahi jeera*)
250 gm poppy seeds (*khus khus*)
250 gm mustard seeds
250 gm roasted chickpeas
250 gm wheat
125 gm black pepper
50 gm cinnamon sticks
10 gm cardamom
10 gm cloves
10 gm star anise (badian)
10 gm pepper leaves (*tirphal*)
10 gm cassia buds (nagkesar)
10 gm mace (*javitri*)
10 gm mugwort (*maipatri*)
10 gm nutmeg (*jaiphal*)
10 gm all spice

METHOD

Dry roast each of the given ingredients separately on low heat. Once roasted, grind the ingredients into a fine powder. Bottle masala is red in colour. Since it tends to lose its colour and potency with age, it is necessary to store it in a good airtight container and note down the date. If stored in a brown beer bottle, it can last for a year.

RECHAD MASALA

In Portuguese, the word "recheado" literally means stuffed, filled or rammed. The description rechad or rechado masala is derived from there. It is a pungent and tangy, red marinade that is used to stuff fish, like mackerel or pomfret, in a local fry up that defines Goan taste and cuisine.

Rechad masala is fiery hot, flaming red and aromatically intoxicating. It is a combination of all the flavours that are an essential part of most Goan cooking. Most Goan homes have created their own variations. After a bit of digging, I found this recipe to be a good balance between the traditional and the easy. For those of you who have the courage to experiment, you can try marinating chicken or other meat with this masala and then, either make a sukka or a barbeque.

RECIPE

10 mins

 Serves 6–8

 marinating fish, prawns or chicken

INGREDIENTS

200 gm Kashmiri red chillies

1 onion

1 head of garlic

100 gm ginger

10 cloves

10 peppercorns

5 cinnamon sticks

½ tsp cumin seeds (*jeera*)

1 tbsp sugar

Tamarind pulp

½ cup vinegar

1 tsp salt

METHOD

In a mixer or blender, add the red chillies, garlic, ginger, cloves, pepper, cinnamon, cumin seeds, onion, sugar, salt, tamarind pulp and half a cup of vinegar. Grind the spices with vinegar in the mixer or blender to a fine paste. Store the rechad masala in airtight containers.

The masala can be used immediately to marinate fish and prawns. It can be refrigerated and stored for a month or so.

INDEX

A

Abeda's Nihari, 98-9, *98*

Akki Roti, 36-7, *37*

Akoori on Toast, 52-3, *53*

Aloo Parantha Tadkewala, 40-1, *40*

Anday ka Halwa, 128

B

Beef, 110-1, *110*

Bhindi Fatafat, 20-1, *20*

Bhopali Roti, 38

Bombay Chicken Curry, 73

Bottle Masala, 142

Brinjal Fritter, 16-7, *16*

C

Channe ka Pulao, 28-9, *29*

Charcharleli Batati, 48-9, *48*

Chicken Pasta Curry, 70-1, *71*

Chicken, 62-3, *62*

Chinchoni, 82-3, *83*

Chorizro Pulao with Dry Fruits, 116-7, *117*

Chutney, 132

Croissant Pudding, 126-7, *126*

D

Dessert, 118-9, *118*

Double Bean Sukka, 27

E

Eddie's Mutton Stew, 108-9, *108*

Egg Fried Mutton Chops, 100-1, *101*

Egg, 50-1, *50*

Esperanza's Chicken Curry, 64-5, *65*

F

Fish Kujit, 84

Fish, 76-7, *76*

Fugias, 58-9, *58*

G

Ginger Garlic Chutney, 133

Goan Egg Drop Curry, 60-1, *60*

Goan Potato Curry, 44-5, *45*

Gomes Cafreal, 74-5, *75*

Green Kheema, 96-7, *97*

H

Hingatelache Vatane, 43

I

Indian Scotch Egg Curry, 58-9, *59*

K

Kaju Chicken Korma, 66-7, *66*

Kashmiri Pundit Dum Aloo, 24-5, *25*

Kerala Beef Fry, 115

Kheema Parantha, 94-5, *94*

Kori (Chicken) Sukka, 72

L

Lagan nu Achaar, 135

M

Madras Onion Sambar, 26

Masalas, 140-9, *140*

Mince Potato Chops with Mint, 107

Mutton do Piaza, 104-5, *104*

Mutton Khuddi, 106-7

Mutton, 90-1, *90*

P

Pakistani Dal Tadka, 30-1, *30*

Pakistani Pot Roast Fillets, 112-3, *113*

Pakoda Dahi Kadi, 46-7

Panchamrut Drink, 139, *139*

Pathare Prabhu Chutney, 138

Pear Chutney, 134, *134*

Phodnichi Poli, 22

Pizza Sunny Side Up, 54-5, *54*

Pomfret Moile, 78-9, *78*

Prawn & Drumstick Curry, 88-9, *88*

Prawn Pathwad, 85

Prawns Atwan, 80-1, *80*

Rechad Masala, 141

S

Sev Badam Burfi, 120-1, *120*

Shikari Pulao, 92-3, *93*

Sides, 130-1, *130*

T

Tamilian Kotthu Parantha, 18

Tipsy Pudding, 122-3

V

Vanilla Sheermal, 124

Varias, 39

Vegetarian, 14-5, *14*

JAICO PUBLISHING HOUSE

ESTABLISHED IN 1946, Jaico Publishing House is home to world-transforming authors such as Sri Sri Paramahansa Yogananda, Osho, The Dalai Lama, Sri Sri Ravi Shankar, Robin Sharma, Deepak Chopra, Jack Canfield, Eknath Easwaran, Devdutt Pattanaik, Khushwant Singh, John Maxwell, Brian Tracy and Stephen Hawking.

Our late founder Mr. Jaman Shah first established Jaico as a book distribution company. Sensing that independence was around the corner, he aptly named his company Jaico ('Jai' means victory in Hindi). In order to service the significant demand for affordable books in a developing nation, Mr. Shah initiated Jaico's own publications. Jaico was India's first publisher of paperback books in the English language.

While self-help, religion and philosophy, mind/body/spirit and business titles form the cornerstone of our non-fiction list, we publish an exciting range of travel, current affairs, biography and popular science books as well. Our renewed focus on popular fiction is evident in our new titles by a host of fresh, young talent from India and abroad. Jaico's recently established Translations Division translates selected English content into nine regional languages.

Jaico's Higher Education Division (HED) is recognized for its student-friendly textbooks in Business Management and Engineering which are in use countrywide.

In addition to being a publisher and distributor of its own titles, Jaico is a major national distributor of books of leading international and Indian publishers. With its headquarters in Mumbai, Jaico has branches and sales offices in Ahmedabad, Bangalore, Bhopal, Bhubaneswar, Chennai, Delhi, Hyderabad, Kolkata and Lucknow.